A PLUME BOOK

HARMLESS AS DOVES

Calais Photography

PAUL LOUIS GAUS lives with his wife, Madonna, in Wooster, Ohio, just a few miles north of Holmes County, where the world's largest and most varied settlement of Amish and Mennonite people is found. His knowledge of the culture of the "Plain People" stems from more than thirty years of extensive exploration of the narrow blacktop roads and lesser gravel lanes of this pastoral community, which includes several dozen sects of Anabaptists living closely among the so-called English or Yankee non-Amish people of the county. Paul lectures widely about the Amish people he has met and about the lifestyles, culture, and religion of this remarkable community of Christian pacifists. He can be found online at: www.plgaus.com. He also maintains a Web presence with Mystery Writers of America: www.mysterywriters.org.

Other Amish-Country Mysteries by P. L. Gaus

Blood of the Prodigal

Broken English

Clouds Without Rain

Cast a Blue Shadow

A Prayer for the Night

Separate from the World

HARMLESS AS DOVES

AN AMISH-COUNTRY MYSTERY

P. L. GAUS

A PLUME BOOK

PLUME
Published by the Penguin Group
Penguin Group (USA) Inc., 375 Hudson Street, New York, New York 10014, U.S.A. • Penguin Group (Canada), 90 Eglinton Avenue East, Suite 700, Toronto, Ontario, Canada M4P 2Y3 (a division of Pearson Penguin Canada Inc.) • Penguin Books Ltd., 80 Strand, London WC2R 0RL, England • Penguin Ireland, 25 St. Stephen's Green, Dublin 2, Ireland (a division of Penguin Books Ltd.) • Penguin Group (Australia), 250 Camberwell Road, Camberwell, Victoria 3124, Australia (a division of Pearson Australia Group Pty. Ltd.) • Penguin Books India Pvt. Ltd., 11 Community Centre, Panchsheel Park, New Delhi – 110 017, India • Penguin Group (NZ), 67 Apollo Drive, Rosedale, Auckland 0632, New Zealand (a division of Pearson New Zealand Ltd.) • Penguin Books (South Africa) (Pty.) Ltd., 24 Sturdee Avenue, Rosebank, Johannesburg 2196, South Africa

Penguin Books Ltd., Registered Offices: 80 Strand, London WC2R 0RL, England

Published by Plume, a member of Penguin Group (USA) Inc. Reprinted by arrangement with Ohio University Press.

ISBN 978-1-62090-344-5

Printed in the United States of America

PUBLISHER'S NOTE
This is a work of fiction. Names, characters, places, and incidents are either the product of the author's imagination or are used fictitiously, and any resemblance to actual persons, living or dead, business establishments, events, or locales is entirely coincidental.

Dedicated to my mother, Ollie Marie (Mrs. Robert Louis) Gaus, who has asked me several times to tell what became of Sara Yoder after her rescue in *A Prayer for the Night.*

Preface and Acknowledgments

SALT CREEK Township Lane 601, in north-central Holmes County, Ohio, skirts a crest overlooking a wide pastoral valley in the hills south of Fredericksburg, and on a three-mile stretch of that simple country lane, one finds a curious assortment of Amish farms and English homes. The mix of cultures is fascinating, and the range and variety of religious persuasions among the Plain People is likely to be surprising to those who have not frequently traveled the region. Like much of the rest of Holmes County, this is a place set thoroughly apart, and typical of most complex religious tapestries, there is great variety among the various Schwartzentruber and Old Order Amish peoples who live there.

The Amish enterprises on this short stretch of road are also greatly varied. There is a sawmill, a carpenter's shop, a stove factory, a harness shop, a sewing shop, an old gasoline engine repair shop, and two one-room parochial schools, one nearly eighty years old and the other quite new and modern, in a peculiarly *Amish modern* way. Cars, trucks, and horse-drawn buggies, surreys, hacks, and wagons share the road on any given day, and occasionally in summer, one sees kids out with pony carts, too, pacing along serenely, where little of the spectacle of modern America ever intrudes. In fact, it is so quiet and remote there that the high ground to the south is still a good place to see the night stars, because there are so few electric lights to dim the display of the heavens. So, this sheltered corner of Holmes County seemed to me to be the perfect place to set this story, with characters who rarely get to town, who rarely have any contact with the ignoble circus of modern American culture, and who typically have scant knowledge of modern law enforcement protocols involving arrest and Miranda warnings.

For the portion of the story that takes place in greater Sarasota and Manatee Counties, Florida, I am indebted for hospitality to David and Ann Chatlain, as well as for nautical expertise to Seaman Richard M. Royal, BM3, U.S. Coast Guard, Cortez Station. I also thank Laura McKee for spiritual insight.

But my greatest thanks go to David Sanders, who mercifully convinced me to abandon the first draft of this story and start completely anew. Over the years, his insights into my stories and characters have been a steadfast and accomplished source of instruction and inspiration.

Behold, I send you forth as
sheep in the midst of wolves:
be ye therefore wise as serpents
and harmless as doves.

Matthew 10:16

HARMLESS AS DOVES

1

Wednesday, October 7
4:30 A.M.

WELL BEFORE dawn, Bishop Leon D. Shetler was coaxed from sleep by the whispers of his morning chores, and he rose up and sat on the edge of his bed, honoring his custom of thanking God for the peace that rested over his household. He knew that the worries of leadership would soon find him, but for the moment, as he sat in the dark, the blessings of his life were the focus of his thoughts. It was like that every morning for him. There was peace before daylight, and as was his habit, he sat still for a long moment to enjoy it.

Beside him, Katie stirred in her sleep and then settled deeper into her pillow. She was as familiar to him as his own thoughts, as comfortable in his life as his most intimate prayers, and he thanked God for her, wondering how many men still knew to thank God for their wives. He tried to teach the men about this at the Sunday meetings, but he often asked himself how many of them really understood.

As he sat and prayed, he felt a cool draft over his toes, the night air spilling in over the sill, and he wondered how many men knew to let their houses breathe this way, with the health of fresh air drifting in through the screens.

In his stocking feet, he eased down the cherry-wood staircase to the kitchen, drawing his sleeping shirt around him. Sure of his way in the dark, he stepped to the wooden counter, took a match from a canister, and stroked it against the metal dome of his red kerosene milking lantern. Once he had the flame guttering with new life, he adjusted the wick and set the lantern on the counter. Then as the lantern threw soft light into the kitchen, he rubbed the sleeve of his blouse and asked himself silently how many men still knew the blessings of silk, sleeping in the garments their wives had made—a soft blouse, sleeping pants of cotton, and socks of warm wool?

He had tried to teach his men about this, too. But how many men understood these blessings? How many men still knew to thank God for their wives in this peaceful time of the day, before the worries of life pressed forward in the mind?

Striking another match, Bishop Shetler lit a fire in the front chamber of his cast-iron woodstove, and the aromatic smoke from the walnut kindling lifted a pleasant aroma into the cold kitchen air. At the aluminum sink, he pumped the black spigot handle several times and rinsed soot from his knuckles, using the sulfur water from the well beneath the house. Back at the counter, he sliced an orange on the wood block and stood at the kitchen window to bite into a wedge, thinking it a marvel that this orange had been hanging on a tree in Pinecraft, Florida, only a week ago. But why should he marvel? The congregation had arranged for the bus driver to bring him a box of oranges every week, and he was only too happy to accept the gesture. After all, the gift of fresh fruit was scant compensation for the duties he shouldered as bishop.

Maybe this year he and Katie would go to Pinecraft and pick their own oranges. Blue skies, palm trees, and the white sand beaches nearby. Just a week in Pinecraft, like everyone else. Twenty-four hours on a Pioneer Trails bus to Sarasota, and they'd be slicing the oranges they'd picked themselves. They'd ride the city bus out to the beach. Everybody said Lido Beach was the best. Less crowded than Siesta. Just an easy bus ride over the causeway bridge, and he and Katie would be wading in the surf, while snow blanketed the ground in Ohio. And they'd ride those large tricycles there, all around among the cottages and trailers, visiting with folk from the Amish settlements up north, lounging on chairs in the sun, and meeting the bus each day to see who else had just made the trip down. Yes, Pinecraft is the Amish place for winters, the bishop reckoned. They could bunk in with relatives—everybody knows someone down there—and take their time with each sunny day, letting the ocean breezes stir through their hair.

But what nonsense, Leon thought. What vanity. Of course you'll never go. The people—*the Gemie*—the church needs you here. Your duties are clear. And why complain? You have fresh oranges—all you can eat—so let it be, old Leon, let it be.

Finished with his orange and shaking his head at his dreams of Pinecraft, the bishop poured hot water into a coffee mug. He spooned instant coffee into the water, stirred it twice around with a callused finger, and carried it out to the mudroom in back. There, he took his first sip and set the coffee mug on a shelf. Then he stuffed his stockinged feet and sleeping pants into the legs of his denim dungarees—his wife had made those, too—and he swung his shoulders through his suspenders, pulled on a denim waistcoat, and set his black felt hat on his head.

When he had wiggled his feet into his muck boots, he pushed through the back door into the night air, chuckled over his forgetfulness, and turned back inside to retrieve the lantern and his coffee mug. But he noticed that he'd left the door on the woodstove hanging open in front, so he set the lantern down on the porch floor and walked back into the kitchen, where he closed the door of the stove to temper the flames.

No point wasting wood, he thought. Let it burn slowly until Katie wakes up. As cold as it was these days, she'd appreciate the fire in the stove. The kitchen would be warmed up in no time at all, if puttering old fools didn't leave the stove door hanging open in front of the flames.

Outside behind the big house, Shetler headed for the barn with his coffee and lantern in hand, and as he drew near to the barn, he heard Hedda, already in her stall, stomping to be milked. Impatient in her old age, he thought. She was his last milking cow.

Once his dairy herd had numbered in the dozens. His spread was as big as anyone's. But he had drawn the lot, and God's calling had settled upon him. He had decided to disperse his herd in order to attend to his new duties as bishop. But old Hedda he had kept. Hedda for her sweet milk. And to preserve his illusions, he chuckled, that he was still only a simple, peasant farmer, and not the leader of all his people.

Nosed into her milking stall, Hedda stamped her feet again as he walked up to her with his lantern. He took his three-legged milking stool down from a peg and dropped it onto the straw-covered floor, beside her back feet. After he had positioned his milking pail under her udder, he warmed his hands on the coffee mug, and as he stroked the milk from her, Bishop Shetler remembered the other cows he had tended in his years on the farms. First as a lad on his father's sprawling farm, then on this smaller section, once his father's original spread had been divided among the sons. Now Shetler's nearest neighbors were his own brothers and their families. The other people of his district had the outlying farms, with a few English souls sprinkled into the mix, all of it straddling Salt Creek Township Lane 601, in the hill country south of Fredericksburg, Ohio. Salt Creek South, his district was called. Thirty-five families with the one-room schoolhouse for their young scholars. A cemetery, a sawmill, two furniture shops, an engine repair shop, a sewing machine concern, a buggy shop, and a wheel factory, plus a harness shop and two blacksmiths.

As he milked, the bishop's mind turned toward his duties, and as the peacefulness of his morning thoughts faded, he remembered again that there were English in the valley, too. Just a few, but some of them were rare characters. Like Billy and Darba Winters—Billy a conspiracy theory nut, and Darba half troubled in her own way. She kept that Rumspringe room in her barn, for the Amish kids running wild, and Shetler knew he'd have to challenge that, someday. Trouble was, the kids were going to run wild sometime, and maybe a safe place to do that was what they needed most. Maybe he should just look the other way. If he never brought it up, he'd never have to rule against it. So, maybe the better wisdom was just to let it be. At least for now.

And remember, the bishop thought, that Katie liked Darba Winters, and she cared for her in her "blue" times. She sat with Darba in her periods of "negativity." Leon didn't understand Darba's troubles entirely, but he respected Katie's instincts to care for her, and when Darba had needed someone other than her psychiatrist to talk to, Katie had proved as good a listener as anyone. Katie was good for Darba, and Bishop Shetler knew to let that be, too. Darba had been a fine teacher, and she deserved a good friend to talk to.

Then there was Glenn Spiegle, a new convert to Amish ways but, truth be told, little more than a wayward drunk from Florida, who hadn't yet confessed all of his sorrows. A man who couldn't yet speak of his deepest remorse. But Shetler had accepted him, and so had the congregation. Spiegle had taken a pledge to stop drinking, moved to Holmes County, studied with Shetler, and been baptized—converted to Amish life by the guilt he carried forward from his past, and by the testimony of peacefulness that he had witnessed in the brethren in Pinecraft, in the eastern suburbs of Sarasota.

But remember, the bishop thought, that it was Billy Winters who had brought him up here. Yes, acknowledge that, Old Leon. Conspiracy nut though he was, Billy Winters had still managed to dry Glenn Spiegle out after prison, and he had brought him up to Ohio two years ago in his truck. Now Spiegle lives righteously among us—because of the friendship of Billy Winters—and the bishop wondered how many men would make that much of a difference in another man's life.

But there was also trouble in that redemption story. Spiegle had money. Cash money, and a lot of it. He'd agreed to pay an *English* price for an Amish farm, and it had been my decision, Leon mused, whose land he would buy—Mony Detweiler's and not Jacob Miller's.

But now Leon realized he should have foreseen the trouble. He should have known that the allure of riches would snare the greedy man first. He should have known that Jacob Miller, always quick to perceive a slight and far too interested in his personal prosperity, would never get over the loss of all that money. It wouldn't matter in the least to Jacob Miller that Mony Detweiler's duty was to hold that money for the district, as an emergency fund. For hospital bills. For the property taxes. For new land purchases for the young lads who would need farms in order to start their own families. It was money that was already spoken for, and Detweiler could never spend it on his own. He was obliged by the bishop's instructions to hold the money in reserve, to be used only for the good of the people.

Miller's daughter Vesta was another concern. Such a beautiful girl. So many suitors. Evidently she had chosen a boy—Crist Burkholder. They had been to see Shetler already, to have their first marriage consultations with their bishop. They'd be a fine couple. Vesta Miller was to marry Crist Burkholder in March, before the spring plantings, when all the families could attend.

It was all arranged, it seemed, but then Jacob Miller couldn't accept it. He wanted Vesta to marry Glenn Spiegle, a man twice her age. Miller the bullish authoritarian, insisting that Vesta was only seventeen, and that he was still the ruler of his own household. The *scriptural head of his family,* the bishop sighed. So, that was another long, hard conversation that awaited him today—to teach Jacob Miller the deeper truths about a father's authority.

You've already chastised him enough, Shetler thought as he milked. Time for sterner words. Take Jacob Miller aside today, and warn him one last time.

Behind him, Shetler heard a rustling in the straw. When he turned on his milking stool, he saw young Crist Burkholder standing behind him, head down, hat in hand, grief in all his features.

When he saw Burkholder's face, Shetler stood and turned, asking, "What's wrong?"

Burkholder shook his head and shrugged fatalistically. "You know Herr Spiegle wants to marry Vesta Miller?"

"Yes, I've heard that, Crist. But I reckon that I'm still bishop. I reckon that I'll have something to say about that."

"Doesn't matter, now, Bischoff. Vesta isn't going to be able to marry me or Spiegle."

"Why, Crist? What's wrong?"

"I just killed Glenn Spiegle."

* * *

Bishop Shetler pulled Crist Burkholder out of the barn, and Crist tried to follow on legs that were stiff and unresponsive. His mind was the same—stiff and frozen—processing thoughts only sluggishly, giving him mostly the surreal flashes of a nightmare he himself had just created.

There was a brief glimpse of Vesta Miller's eyes, hopeful yesterday. Happy. Then he imagined how her face would twist in disgust, once she knew that the man she had pledged to marry was now a murderer. Lost, outcast, frozen.

Crist tried to command his legs to move as the bishop pulled him out into the dawn air, but his mind gave him no encouragement in the task, and his legs produced only a feeble stutter step, like the Tin Man in that Oz movie.

Strange that you're thinking of that. Funny. That Tin Man, frozen in place without his oilcan. Couldn't get his legs to move. In that Wizard movie we saw. In Crazy Darba's Rumspringe room.

"Crist, tell me what happened."

"I hit him. As hard as I could. Can't remember."

One good swing, and he dropped at my feet like a limp rope.

They were out under the stars now, and Crist still couldn't get his legs to cooperate with the bishop's intentions.

"Stand right here, Crist," the bishop was saying.

Cold night air, still as death. Light beginning to break at dawn. Oilcans and the Tin Man. Maybe the Scarecrow, too, with a useless, frozen brain. A head full of straw. Why can't you think, Crist Burkholder? Hooves pounding out through the barn door, the clatter of wooden wheels on a hack trailing behind it.

"Crist, climb up!"

But Crist Burkholder was frozen by a singular mental clarity—dead Glenn Spiegle, in a crumpled heap at his feet.

"Crist! We've got to call the sheriff."

"What?" *Vesta is waiting for me.* "Crazy Darba saw me."

"Stop calling her that, Crist," the bishop scolded. "Climb up. We've got to get to a phone."

Nervous tension broke in Burkholder's throat as a strangled croak, and the bishop shouted down from the hack, "Wait!" and jumped down from his seat to run back into the barn.

This was to be our day of emancipation. Vesta and me. Does she know by now? Darba Winters saw me run away. So, Vesta surely knows by now that I am a murderer.

"Here, Crist," the bishop said behind him. "Sit down on this stool."

Sit? Sure. Ease down on your Tin Man knees.

As Burkholder tried to lower himself to the milking stool, the old bishop failed to guide him down, and Burkholder lost his balance, struck the edge of the seat, and toppled onto the packed soil in front of the barn doors. Shetler set the lantern on the ground beside Burkholder's head and tried to sit him up. But the strapping farm boy, built like a sturdy oak and twice the size of the old bishop, lay stiff and unmovable on the ground, and before the bishop could get a good grasp on his shoulders, Burkholder pulled his knees up to his chest and wrapped his arms around them, thinking, *I'm the Tin Man.*

And I just killed the only man who could have taken Vesta away from me.

So, that's what the sheriff will think. What everyone will think.

That I killed a man over Vesta Miller, because her father just couldn't let it be. That he just couldn't let Vesta marry a simple farm boy, when so rich an eligible man lived right among us.

2

Wednesday, October 7
6:00 A.M.

THE BISHOP ran back toward the house shouting, "Katie! Katie, wake up!"

He hurtled two steps at a time up into the mudroom and dashed into the kitchen, where Katie was standing at the sink, holding a half-peeled orange, head turned in his direction.

"Katie!" he shouted, waving her forward, "Help!" Then he ran back outside.

Barefooted, and dressed only in her pink sleeping gown and blue quilted robe, Katie followed her husband out into the backyard. There the bishop knelt at Burkholder's head and rocked him by his rounded shoulders, trying to secure a grip on the lad. Katie knelt at Burkholder's side and pushed against his elbows, which were locked in place over his knees, and together the Shetlers managed to roll Crist onto his back.

Burkholder's arms slipped from his knees, and his legs straightened. He lay flat in the dirt, his eyes popping open and then closed, as if he were testing his vision, coming up from a deep sleep.

The bishop bent over Burkholder and asked, "Crist, are you sure he's dead?" and Katie drew a startled breath, stood up, and cried out, "Who?"

Shaking Burkholder to rouse him, the bishop said to Katie, "Crist says he killed Glenn Spiegle." He wedged his hands under the boy's shoulders and heaved him up to a sitting position, adding, "He says he struck Spiegle in a fight, and Spiegle fell dead."

With her fingers laid across her lips to stifle a cry, Katie stood stiffly beside her husband. Stunned, she asked, "Are you sure he's really dead?"

Coming somewhat back into awareness, Burkholder focused his eyes on the bishop's face and said, "I felt his neck. Like they do on the TV."

Shetler positioned himself behind Burkholder and braced him under his arms to help him up onto his knees. Then Burkholder stood to full height, two heads taller than either of the Shetlers, and wobbling on his unsteady legs, he stepped to the hack in front of the barn doors and leaned over to plant his forearms on the buckboard seat, head hanging down.

"Where is he?" Katie asked at Burkholder's side. "Where is Glenn Spiegle?"

"Inside Crazy Darba's barn," Burkholder muttered. "Just outside the Rum Room. I left him lying in a heap. On the concrete pad. Right where he fell."

Then with sorrow cast in his eyes, Burkholder turned to Katie and asked, "Do you think Vesta knows by now?"

"I don't know, Crist," Katie said, laying a gentle hand on his arm. "News travels. Have you told anyone else?"

"No," Burkholder said. "But Darba saw me running up her drive."

"Will she know to check in the barn?" the bishop asked.

Crist shrugged. "I left my Chevy running. With the lights on. So maybe she'll go down there."

"I need to go to Darba," Katie said. "She's gonna need some help today."

The bishop disagreed. "No, Katie. We need to find a phone."

"You two can do that, while I check on Darba."

"No, Katie. I need you to get the Burkholders."

"OK, but I can do both."

The bishop hesitated, and then nodded. "Which phone should I let on that I know about?"

Katie thought. "You know there are a lot of cell phones. If people were aware of that, you'd have to pass a ruling."

"I was thinking about Mony's phone. In the woods behind his barns."

"If he knows that you know about that phone," Katie said, "he'll expect you to tell him to take it down."

"But I do know about his phone," the bishop complained. "And I know about all the cell phones, too."

"Are you ready to rule against all the cell phones?" Katie asked.

"I don't know," the bishop said, shaking his head. "Probably not yet."

"Then use Mony Detweiler's phone in the woods. You can think about the cell phones later."

* * *

With Crist Burkholder on the buckboard seat at his side, Bishop Shetler whipped his horse out onto Township Lane 601 and turned south to descend the high hill where the Shetler farm commanded a view of the wide pastoral valley of the Salt Creek South district. Shetler kept after his horse with an impatient whip, and a half mile later, he turned right to drop over a ridge into the long drive that cut the wide fields of Mony Detweiler's farm, on a west-facing slope between 601 and the narrow creek far down in the timbered bottoms.

As he pulled to a stop in front of the Detweilers' white frame house, Shetler shouted out, "Mony!" and climbed down, stepped around, and eased Burkholder down from the buckboard.

The front door opened, and a stocky woman in a plain rose dress and white lace apron stepped out onto the front porch, holding a kitchen towel and a white china plate that she was drying.

Shetler called up to her. "Lizzie, I need to use Mony's phone."

Other than the slight arching of an eyebrow, Lizzie Detweiler displayed no surprise. Circumspectly, she said, "Mony's out in the barn, Bischoff."

Shetler scolded, "I know about the phone, Lizzie," turning to round the corner of the house with Burkholder in tow.

When the bishop confronted Mony Detweiler in the barn about his phone, the thin Amishman showed only a faint disappointment at losing his secret. When Shetler explained why he needed to use the phone, Detweiler took a sympathetic step toward Crist Burkholder, and then waved the two men forward, setting a hurried pace through the back doors of the barn, out into the woods behind.

Young Burkholder and Bishop Shetler followed Detweiler along a trail for nearly a hundred yards through the timber, coming at last to a small glade, where an old-fashioned black dial phone was mounted on a wooden shelf fastened to the broad trunk of a maple tree. A small, shingled roof with sideboards sheltered the phone.

Taking the lead, Detweiler stepped up to the phone, spun the dial through a nine and two ones, and held the phone receiver out for the bishop. Shetler took the phone, held it to his ear tentatively, and then pressed the earpiece closer to listen, saying, "Yes, I have an emergency. One of my boys has killed a man. Glenn Spiegle."

Then Burkholder and Detweiler heard the bishop answer several questions from the 911 operator:

"No, Crist Burkholder. It is Glenn Spiegle who has been killed."

"Crist has told me only that he struck Glenn Spiegle in a fight, and that Spiegle is dead."

"In Darba Winters's barn, on Township Lane 601."

"Yes, Township 601. The Billy and Darba Winters residence."

"It's the brick ranch home, across the road from the Spiegle farm."

"Really? How did that happen so fast?"

"OK, we'll go there now."

"Yes, tell the sheriff we will be there in ten minutes."

"No, Crist says openly that he did it."

"No, not really."

"OK, but please tell the sheriff that we are coming there now, so that Crist can turn himself in for the murder."

When he handed the phone back to Mony Detweiler, Bishop Shetler said, "The sheriff is already at Darba's place. There's a bit of a crowd out front on the lane, and the sheriff is down in the barn with the coroner."

Hesitating, the bishop added, "They're expecting us, so we should get going."

Crist fell in behind Detweiler, who led the men back up the trail, with the bishop following after Crist. The morning light was stronger now, casting long shadows behind the tall hickory, walnut, and maple trees of the wood. The splashes of fall color overhead were backlit by the sunlight, giving a red-orange glow to the trail. Leaves already down crunched underfoot, and the acorns and twigs cracked and popped as the men paced along, Burkholder whispering, "I need to talk to Vesta."

Behind him, the bishop said, "First, Crist, you need to tell the sheriff exactly what you did. There'll be plenty of time to talk to Vesta, after that."

Stopping to turn back to the bishop, Burkholder asked, "What makes you think she will come to see me in jail?"

Thinking compassion appropriate where encouragement wasn't reasonable, Shetler took Burkholder by the shoulders, and said gently, "I'll bring her down to see you, Crist. Once she is ready to talk."

Privately, Shetler wondered, How many bishops do you know, Old Leon, who would know what to do now?

3

Wednesday, October 7
7:00 A.M.

THE BISHOP drove Crist back to the Shetler farm on the high ground along 601. In the kitchen, they found a note from Leon's wife. Shetler read the short note and handed it to Burkholder. Crist read it while the bishop pulled a pitcher of fresh milk out of the heavy wooden icebox beside the pantry:

> Leon—I have gone to get the Burkholders.
> I will meet you at Darba's place. I finished
> milking Hedda. You should eat something.

Shetler poured two glasses of milk and handed one to Burkholder, saying, "You should eat something."

While Crist sipped milk, the bishop pulled two oranges out of the crate under the kitchen sink and handed one to Burkholder. Crist set his glass on the counter and absently rolled the orange in his fingers. The bishop took it back, pierced the peel with his thumbnail, worked some of the peel loose, and handed it back to Burkholder. "You can eat that in the hack. On the way to see the sheriff."

* * *

A mile north on 601, the bishop pulled his horse left into Darba Winters's drive and stopped at the top of the slope that led down to Darba's red barn. The coroner's wagon was parked in front of the barn doors, which were closed.

At the top of the drive, Deputy Stan Armbruster stroked a palm over the nose of the bishop's buggy horse and then stepped to the side to talk.

Shetler said, "We need to see the sheriff. This is Crist Burkholder."

Armbruster keyed his shoulder mic and said, "Crist Burkholder is here." Below at the barn, a small door swung open, and Sheriff Bruce Robertson and Sergeant Ricky Niell stepped outside to wave Shetler and Burkholder down the long drive.

Abruptly, Burkholder leapt off the buckboard seat of the hack and started down the drive with a determined gait, shouting, "I did it. I killed him."

Robertson started up the drive with Niell, and they met Burkholder halfway. Holding out his wrists for cuffs, Burkholder confessed again, saying, "I killed him. I killed Glenn Spiegle."

Gently, Robertson pushed Burkholder's hands down and said, "We've no need for that, Crist. Not yet."

"I did it. I killed him."

"I know," Robertson said. "Can we ask you some questions? In the barn?"

By now, Bishop Shetler had pulled his rig off to the side, and he joined the men on the gravel drive. The four men turned for the barn, with Robertson leading and Ricky Niell following after Burkholder and Shetler.

Inside the barn, Coroner Missy Taggert had set up three stands with bright floodlights powered by batteries on the ground. Lying in the focused beams of the lights, on the concrete slab behind a powder-blue Chevy Bellaire, was a prone body, covered with a long tarp.

The shock of seeing the covered body caused Crist Burkholder to double over at the waist, and he turned into a corner of the barn and began to vomit up milk and bits of orange.

Deputy Pat Lance, working beside the body with Missy Taggert, stood up and walked over to Crist, offering him a towel for his mouth. She laid her hand gently on his back, and Crist straightened up at her touch and pulled away, seeming shamed by his weakness. Lance, a stocky, blond Germanic woman in uniform, handed the towel to Burkholder and took a step back to give him some space for his embarrassment.

Ricky stepped over and said, "Crist, we want you to look at the body. Tell us what you did."

"I can't do that!" Crist cried out. Doubling over again, he heaved from his gut.

The bishop said, "I can look," and moved to Taggert's side.

Coroner Taggert, kneeling by the head, lifted the tarp for Shetler, and Shetler looked down, gasped, and stepped back. "That's Glenn Spiegle. He's got the farm across the road."

In the corner, Crist groaned, "I killed him," and straightened up. He used one end of Lance's towel to wipe his lips and the other end to dry his eyes. "I hit him as hard as I could, and he dropped straight down."

Robertson stepped up to Burkholder and asked, "Why did you fight, Mr. Burkholder?"

"We fought about Vesta Miller. He said he wanted to marry her, and he knew I was going to."

"That's all?" Robertson asked.

"He said he'd die if he couldn't marry her. Then he offered me fifteen thousand dollars to let her go. He just threw the money into the trunk of my car, so I got mad, and I hit him. After he dropped, I don't remember much, until I was standing in Bishop Shetler's barn."

Ricky Niell's handset chirped, and Armbruster said over the radio, "The bishop's wife has Burkholder's parents up here. Should I send them down?"

Robertson shook his head no, and Ricky said into his handset, "No, Stan. We'll come up there."

Moaning, Crist said, "I don't want to see my parents right now."

To that, Robertson replied, "You stay here with Sergeant Niell, Mr. Burkholder. Consider yourself under arrest. We'll go talk to your parents."

And he waved the bishop outside.

* * *

Wayne and Mary Burkholder stood in plain Amish attire beside their buggy at the top of Darba's drive, and waited for the rotund Sheriff Robertson to struggle up the graveled slope. After he had managed the climb, Robertson took out a handkerchief and wiped perspiration from his brow, saying, "I'm sorry about this, folks, but Crist has confessed to killing Glenn Spiegle, and I have placed him under arrest."

Bishop Shetler crossed the drive to stand with the Burkholders, and said, "He's down in the barn, Wayne. He says quite plainly that he did it."

Crying, and holding a kerchief to her nostrils, Mary Burkholder asked, "Can we see him, Sheriff?"

"Not just yet. I want to take him down to the jail. Get him charged. Then you can talk to him in my office, before we take him to his cell."

Wooden-faced, Wayne Burkholder asked, "Will this take long, Sheriff?"

"Maybe an hour," Robertson said. "We'll try to finish up with our questions just as soon as we can."

On the lane behind them, there was the clatter of horse's hooves and the rattle of a buggy pulling to a stop in front of the Winters house. They all turned to look, and tiny Vesta Miller, hair tucked up in a loose bun under a bonnet hanging somewhat askew, jumped down out of the buggy before it had come to a stop. The horse angled off into the middle of the road, and Vesta ran up waving her cell phone. Showing panic in all of her features, Vesta cried out, "Is it true?" and stopped beside Mary Burkholder to catch her breath.

Wayne Burkholder stepped away to take charge of Vesta's buggy horse, and Mary took Vesta in her arms. "Crist is down in the barn, Vesta. He says he killed Glenn Spiegle."

"No, no, no," Vesta cried and pushed away. "It can't be true. He was supposed to come for me this morning."

"Did he call you?" Robertson asked, eyeing Vesta's phone.

"No, Darba called," Vesta said, looking from face to face, denying what she had heard.

"Did she just call?" Robertson pressed, glancing back at the Winters house.

"Ten minutes ago, I guess," Vesta said. "I want to see Crist."

"I can't let you talk to him right now," Robertson said, and looked to Bishop Shetler.

Shetler stepped forward and said to Vesta, "We can talk to him down at the sheriff's office."

"No!" Vesta shouted, tears coursing her cheeks. "I want to talk to him! I want to talk to him right now."

Mary reached out for Vesta and took her again into her embrace, saying to Robertson, "There has to be some mistake."

Robertson shook his head. "I need to ask him some more questions. But he says he did it."

Wayne Burkholder walked back with Vesta's horse in tow and said, "Who can help us, Leon? What should we do?"

In the distance, they heard a car horn, and they all watched as Pastor Cal Troyer drove up in his gray carpenter's truck and stopped on the blacktop, blocking the road. Cal stepped out in jeans and a work shirt, saying, "Darba called me. Where's Crist?"

Showing some impatience at answering the question again, Robertson said, "We have him down in the barn, with the body of Glenn Spiegle."

"Have you asked him any questions?" Cal asked, confronting the sheriff with his tone.

"Yes, Cal, that's what we do."

"Well, you need to stop," Cal said. "I've hired him a lawyer."

Robertson gave a sigh. "OK, Cal," he said. "Who?"

"Linda Hart."

"That's just great, Cal!" Robertson barked. "You know she's a hothead."

Smiling, Cal said, "She's bested you a time or two."

"She's a hothead, Cal. That's not what Burkholder needs right now."

Cal shook his head. "She's on her way out here. So you'd better not ask any more questions. I want Crist Burkholder to have a lawyer, and I'm telling you that Linda Hart is it."

"I already have his confession, Cal," Robertson said.

"Take me down there, Bruce."

"Can't do that."

"Let me tell Crist not to say anything more."

"I can't take you down there, Cal."

Troyer turned toward Stan Armbruster and said, "Then have your deputy call down on his radio."

Robertson nodded, and Armbruster said into this shoulder mic, "Burkholder has a lawyer, Ricky. Can't ask him any more questions."

"OK," Ricky said over the radio. "But tell the sheriff he needs to see this."

Robertson nodded a question to Armbruster, and Armbruster said into his mic, "What? The sheriff is standing right here."

"Burkholder calls it a Rum Room. Says Darba Winters lets the kids use the room for their Rumspringe wild times."

Robertson urged another question with a nod to Armbruster, and Armbruster said, "What? It's just a room?"

"Not just a room. There's a DVR hooked to a TV. There's a stack of movies. Got a phone here, and a radio. Then there's a laptop with a fax/printer. And a refrigerator full of drinks and a cupboard full of snacks. Then there's a sink, a little stove, a microwave, and coffee pot. There's also a toilet in a little closet."

Robertson shook his head, cast a glance at Darba Winters's front bay window, turned down the drive, and started marching back toward the barn. Cal turned to look at the bay window, too, and there he saw Darba Winters standing with a mug of coffee, looking out at the people gathering on her drive and front lawn.

To the bishop, Cal said, "I guess Darba has called a few people," and the bishop replied, "It's the cell phones, Cal," and walked off toward the Spiegle farm across the road, muttering under his breath about the relentless intrusions into his life from the modern world of gadgets. And if gadgets weren't enough, now murder.

4

Wednesday, October 7
8:30 A.M.

BISHOP SHETLER walked up the Spiegle driveway, marveling at the disparity between the heaviness in his heart and the light, airy clarity of the morning sky. Marveling also at the transition Crist Burkholder was making from life and freedom to loss and incarceration. And although the sky overhead was clear and deep blue as far as his vision could reach, and although the morning air was as crisp and sweet as a cold autumn apple, the bishop could find no joy in any of it.

We should be taking in the feed corn, Shetler thought, trudging along in the gravel. All the families should be together in their fields, cutting the stalks, pitching the ears into the wagons, stacking the stems for winter. And singing with the work, keeping a happy, purposeful pace. Telling the old stories.

But Shetler stopped, turned back, and studied the gathering crowd in front of the Winters place, and he knew little of that joyful harvest would take place today.

No, today was forevermore a murder day, and the sin of an angry heart would taint everything that happened in his district for months to come. Wayne and Mary Burkholder, brokenhearted by their loss. Vesta Miller, abandoned to her father's harsh commands and rulings. Billy Winters, probably still down in Pinecraft on his delivery for the cheese factory. Did he know yet that his best friend was dead? And Darba Winters, fragile at times, today making phone calls to everyone she knew, stuck inside without Billy, the only man who could smooth her through her rough spells.

Yes, Darba would have made a lot of calls. Phone calls to all the cell phones under Amish pillows. A phone call evidently also to Cal Troyer. Making a call to her psychiatrist, the Bishop hoped, because Darba wasn't the sort to bounce easily into a calm frame of mind, even in the best of times. Even with Billy home.

Shetler shook his head, turned back toward the Spiegle house, and continued slowly up the drive. He walked up to the porch, mounted the steps, and reached out for the doorknob just when Jacob Miller pushed the door open from the inside and stepped out onto the porch in front of the startled Shetler.

Fingering his suspenders nervously, Miller said only, "Bishop," as a greeting and appeared to cover his embarrassment at having been discovered by adding officiously, "Have you heard about Glenn Spiegle?"

Shetler answered by a single nod of his head, allowing Miller to stand openly in his pretense of humility.

Miller stammered out a few syllables, and then he said, "I just thought someone should make sure everything was fine over here."

Shetler eyed the big, florid man for several long seconds and said, "You wear your shame badly, Jacob Miller."

Miller's face grew red, and he stared back at the bishop, unable to hide his indignation.

Shetler let him stew a moment longer and then said, "What are you doing here, Jacob?"

"Like I said, Bischoff, just checking."

"It isn't right, Jacob Miller. You're meddling, again."

Miller had no reply.

The bishop had more to say. "We've talked about these things before, Jacob, but I tell you again, as your bishop, that you meddle too much in other men's affairs."

"I just try to be helpful," Miller stammered.

Losing some intensity, Bishop Shetler said more gently, "You're not home enough as it is, Jacob. And the trouble is, when you are home, you provoke your children with your harsh rulings. And you are a trial to your wife's patience."

"I don't see how you'd know anything like that about my children, Bischoff. Has any of them talked to you?"

"No, but Vesta talks to Darba Winters, and Darba talks to my Katie."

Miller considered this and tried to find a comfortable place to put his hands. He eventually hooked his thumbs into his suspenders and stared at his shoes, saying, "Leon, I just thought someone should look after Spiegle's place, considering that he's been murdered. After all, someone will have to work his fields. There's a lot to do here, and bringing in the corn isn't the least of it. Plus the house will go to someone. No point letting it go to ruin."

Shetler stood on the porch and let Miller talk. He wanted him to say whatever he would. To reveal himself fully to God's perception, and to the bishop's. And into the silence, Jacob Miller found it necessary to speak further.

"It's true, Leon," he continued. "We've got to decide who will get Spiegle's farm."

Showing no emotion, Bishop Shetler said, "His will deeds the land to me."

Seeming at first disappointed, Miller hesitated, thought, and said, "Then you will need help deciding who will work the land."

Bishop Shetler shrugged. "Some of the young men will need farms. They are my first concern."

"Or, we could lease the land, Leon. Make a profit."

"Like you lease your land out to *English?*" the bishop asked, still showing no emotion.

Miller nodded self-consciously. They had talked before about this issue, too. "My boys don't need land, Leon. They're earning a fine living making furniture."

"In your shop, Jacob?"

"Yes. It is my shop."

"And you keep the earnings?"

"Of course. Until they marry."

"And your girls make quilts, Jacob. Do you keep those earnings, too?"

"You know what it costs to run a family."

Stepping forward, Shetler looked up into the rheumy eyes of the big Miller and said, "You value money more than you value your family."

Miller stepped back a pace and took an indignant tone. "You know I support the whole congregation, Leon. You know I give my share."

"It's really not about the money, Jacob. It has really never been about the money. I warn you, if you keep provoking your family with your harsh and critical lording . . ."

"Lording?"

"Yes, with your harsh lording-over, you'll end up a bitter, lonely man who can't figure out where to put all the remorse that God will plant in your heart, once you learn the truth of your excesses. The truth of your mistakes."

"Remorse?"

"If God opens your heart to the damage you've done your children with your stern lording-over, your days will end full of remorse, and there won't be anything you can do about it. They'll all be grown and gone."

"Damage? What damage? I provide. And isn't the father the head of his household? A husband the head of his wife?"

"You quote the scriptures badly, and clearly you have no idea what they mean."

"I think I know my Bible as well as the next man."

"Enough! As your bishop, I warn you to change your ways. Your children need your love and approval, more than they need your authority. Vesta, now, most of all."

"What has Vesta got to do with any of this?"

Bishop Shetler stared back at Miller and wanted, with all of his human instincts, to berate the man for the ruin and heartache he had caused his family. But, where he had been considering chastisement, a prayer rose in his mind, and he remembered himself. He remembered his duty as bishop. His duty to instruct. To instruct always by example. Sometimes also with words. His duty to mend, where brokenness arose and festered.

Choosing his words carefully, Shetler asked, "If you had let Vesta marry Crist Burkholder, Jacob, do you really think Glenn Spiegle would be dead?"

5

Wednesday, October 7
8:30 A.M.

WHILE THE bishop was walking up Spiegle's driveway, Cal Troyer caught up with Bruce Robertson on Darba's drive, and he stopped the big sheriff outside the smaller door into the Winterses' barn. The larger double barn doors to the right, built tall and wide to admit farm machinery, were still closed. Robertson was reaching for the doorknob of the smaller door when Cal tapped him on the shoulder.

"Bruce, you need to handle Burkholder carefully. He's Amish."

"No kidding, Cal! I'd never have guessed."

"You know what I mean. He's not going to know anything about arrests. Procedures. Court. You've got to be sure to explain his rights to him."

"You're not his lawyer, Cal," Robertson snapped.

"I told you, Bruce. Linda Hart is coming out. Wait for her."

Robertson opened the door, stepped inside the big barn, and waited for Troyer to follow. The two stood inside, at the edge of the illumination of Missy's floodlights. The contrast between the two men was striking—Robertson, tall and rounded at all the edges by excessive weight, heavy since birth; Troyer, short and lean, muscles evident in his shoulders and arms, fit from his labors as a carpenter. The sheriff was clean shaven, but Troyer had a full white beard. Robertson wore a fifties-style flattop haircut that broadcast his inclination to command, whereas Troyer's hair was long on his neck, suggesting the need for a band to hold it back from his ears. The two men had been friends since kindergarten, although more than occasionally they found themselves on opposite ends of a shouting match, and again today, the tension between them was growing.

Irritated that Troyer was prying again into one of his cases, Robertson called out to Ricky, "Sergeant Niell, where's my prisoner?"

Niell walked over from the back of Burkholder's blue Chevy and said, "He's sitting in the Rum Room, with Pat Lance. We're going to take him into town, as soon as I've gone through his trunk."

"Are you sure that you're allowed to search his trunk?" Cal asked.

Robertson laughed. "You've been watching too much *Law and Order* on TV, Cal."

Ricky explained. "The trunk was wide open when we got here, Cal. Everything was in plain sight."

"Look, folks!" Robertson crowed. "This is a murder scene. We'll search whatever we want."

Not intimidated, Cal asked, "Ricky, have you read him his rights?"

"Oh, for crying out loud!" Robertson shot. "Of course we did!"

Evenly, Ricky said, "Yes, Cal. Just before the bishop left. He heard me do it."

"Are you sure he understands?" Cal asked. "Amish boys won't know a thing about legal matters. Not criminal matters."

"I can't explain everything to him, Cal," Ricky said. "He's got a lawyer coming, right?"

Cal nodded. "Linda Hart."

Impatient with the exchange, Robertson moved to Missy Taggert's side, standing over the body of Glenn Spiegle, and asked, "Missy, you have a time of death?"

Troyer stood his place to listen just inside the barn door, and Ricky resumed his search of the trunk of Burkholder's car.

To Robertson, Missy said, "I just took a liver temperature," and held up her abdomen probe.

"What's that tell us?" Robertson asked, beginning to dump some of his frustration with Cal.

"I need to make some calculations," Missy said, kneeling to clip her temperature probe back into its case. The curls of her brown hair were tucked up inside a medical cap, and she wore a white coat over her slacks and sweater. She stood and explained.

"Darba said she turned the car off when she found the body. But she didn't come down here right away, so it had been running for quite some time."

Robertson interrupted, "She told Ellie on the phone that it wasn't but maybe ten minutes before she came down here. Ten minutes after seeing Burkholder bolt up the drive."

"Point is, Bruce, she did wait. And the car was running. So, that would have warmed it up in here. Warmer than outside, anyway, and when she turned the car off, it would have started cooling down in here. So, we can chart that."

"How?"

"As soon as we got here, Pat Lance started taking ambient temperature readings."

"Way to go, Lance," Robertson said.

"So, we can graph the trend as the barn cooled down. I'll make a few calculations."

"OK, whatever," the sheriff said, already losing interest in the details.

Missy smiled, knowing well her husband's changeabilities. "Give me a couple of hours, Sheriff, and I'll have a time of death for you. Sometime later this afternoon."

"Good," Robertson said and turned to Ricky. "What'd you find, Sergeant?"

At the back of the Chevy, Ricky lifted up a small suitcase, held shut with a leather strap. "This is full of men's clothing. Amish."

Robertson stepped over, peered inside the trunk, and pulled out one of several plastic bottles of commercial spring water. "He was taking a trip," he remarked.

"And there's food in this box," Ricky said, pulling a tab open on a produce box. "Crackers, a jar of peanut butter, boxes of raisins, apples, and candy bars."

Robertson dropped the water bottle back into the trunk and asked, "Did he have any cash on him?"

"About a hundred dollars in an old wallet," Ricky said. "And there was a stack of hundred dollar bills, about fifteen thousand dollars, in the trunk. I bagged it for evidence."

"He claims that's the money he got from Spiegle. You buy that, Ricky?"

Ricky nodded. "He says Spiegle tried to buy him out. To get him to forget about marrying Vesta Miller."

"Can't believe that would work," Robertson commented.

"I think it fits," Ricky said. "Crist says he was leaving to get Vesta this morning. To elope. That's when he says Glenn Spiegle came down and gave him this fifteen thousand, so he wouldn't elope."

"Yeah, sure," Robertson scoffed. "Like fifteen K would have convinced you not to marry Ellie."

Ricky shrugged his shoulders. "It's possible, Sheriff."

"Doesn't make any sense, Ricky. Why would Spiegle think he had a chance with a girl so much younger than him?"

Behind them, the larger barn doors cracked open to admit a shaft of bright morning light, and Linda Hart—lanky in a black pantsuit, with the short, black hair of a tomboy, combed, parted, and gelled in place—pushed the right half of the track doors fully open, and then the left. Then she bent to pick up a black leather briefcase and a can of Diet Pepsi.

"Where's my client, Sheriff?" she asked pleasantly, a wide, toothy smile on her face.

Robertson stepped forward and said, "Linda, don't start."

"Start what, Bruce?"

"You know."

The smile disappeared. "I just want to see my client."

From the back of the Chevy, Ricky said, "He's sitting in the back room."

Hart smiled again and said, "Bruce, if you've mishandled my client, I'll have your head."

"You don't need to make it all adversarial, like this, Hart."

Still smiling, Hart started for the back Rumspringe Room saying, "Everything between us is adversarial, Bruce. You know that."

* * *

While Linda Hart conferred in Darba's Rum Room with Crist Burkholder and the sheriff's people finished up their investigation inside the barn, Cal turned his attention to the cluster of Amish folk standing out on 601, at the top of the Winterses' drive. As he climbed the hill, Cal counted seven black buggies parked along the road in front of the Winters house and three more on the Spiegle side of the road, leaving only a narrow lane for cars to pass down the middle. As he reached the top, a sedan drove slowly through the gap, the English driver and his wife studying the crowd and stopping briefly to peer down the driveway toward the barn.

Not hiding his irritation with their curiosity, Cal waved for them to move on, and the driver pulled forward and stopped in the middle of the road, about forty yards beyond the last buggy. The passenger, a middle-aged lady dressed in a blue cable-knit sweater and a yellow windbreaker, got out and stood beside the car, looking back toward Cal. So Troyer sighed and walked down the lane to her, answered several questions to satisfy her curiosity, and turned back toward Darba's place once the car had driven away.

Back among the Amish people, Cal sought out Vesta Miller and guided her off to the side, seeking privacy between the back of one of the buggies and the wet nose of the horse hitched to the rig behind it. Twisting a white hanky nervously in her slender fingers, Vesta asked Cal, "Where is Crist, Pastor? What are they going to do with him?"

Vesta's white prayer cap was fixed at the back of her head, over the bun of her brown hair, and the white laces of her cap hung straight beside her cheeks, reaching the tops of her shoulders. Her plain aqua dress was tied with a thin cloth string at her waist, and over the dress she wore a white apron. The collar of the dress was plain and unadorned.

At the bottom hem of her dress, an inch of black stockings showed. On her feet she wore plain black walking shoes. The lids of her brown eyes were reddened, and her nose was chafed from wiping it. She struggled not to cry in front of Cal, but she failed in the effort, and more tears spilled onto her cheeks. Weary of using her hanky, Vesta let the tears fall. She asked in a whisper, "What will become of us, Pastor? What will become of Crist and me?"

Some of the other Amish women had wandered close to them, so Cal moved Vesta farther down the road and spoke softly. "He has a good lawyer, Vesta. We need to trust his lawyer now."

"But what are they going to do to him? Will he go to prison?"

"They'll take him to the jail in Millersburg. There's a lot that the sheriff has to do, to charge him and such, so that's why Crist needs a good lawyer. To guide him through the courts."

"Will there be a trial?"

"I don't know, Vesta. We need to let his lawyer work on that. Maybe they won't have a trial."

"Then they'll just put him in prison?"

"We don't know yet."

"Can I talk to him?"

"Maybe down at the jail. Maybe this afternoon. Most likely tomorrow."

Vesta stared down at her shoes. "Right now, I don't know what I'd say to him."

"Maybe tomorrow would be better."

Looking back into Cal's eyes, Vesta asked, "Why didn't he just come to get me? Like we had planned."

"He says that Glenn Spiegle stopped him."

Vesta shook her head, not believing.

Behind them, Bishop Shetler spoke. "Yes, Vesta. Crist said that Glenn Spiegle told him that he would die if he couldn't marry you."

New tears fell over Vesta's cheeks, and she wiped at them with her wrinkled hanky. Cal handed her a folded white handkerchief from his back pocket, and without unfolding it, Vesta held it to her eyes and then to her nose. Then she slipped her wet hanky under the side of her apron and unfolded Cal's handkerchief to blow her nose.

"I'm sorry, Bischoff," she said, "but I never wanted to marry Herr Spiegle."

"I've just spoken with your father," Shetler said. "I know that he's been telling people that you were promised to Spiegle."

"He can't do that," Vesta cried. "I have rights."

"I know," said Shetler. "I've spoken with him about this before. I've warned him several times."

"I can't live at home anymore, Bischoff. He tells us girls that our only duty is to serve a man. He tells us that women are less than men, and it really doesn't matter who we marry. I know he's wrong about women, and I just can't stay there anymore."

"Vesta, I've warned him for the last time, and he knows it."

"But he believes it, Bischoff. He believes that the Bible teaches these things. That men are the bosses of women. And my mother believes it, too. I think she's depressed. I think she's been that way ever since she got married. But I can't live that way. Crist told me I don't have to. I have rights, and women don't have to live that way, anymore."

The bishop considered her words silently, holding Vesta's gaze with his sympathy. Then he said, "The Bible does not teach what your father preaches."

"Somebody needs to tell him that."

"I have told him many times."

"He doesn't listen, Bischoff," Vesta said and looked away.

"But Vesta," the bishop started.

Turning back to face him with obvious disgust, Vesta said, "My sisters are all depressed, Bischoff. They're numb, and they stumble through their chores like scarecrows, because they think life offers them nothing more than what our mother has endured all her married life. I'm sure that they're all depressed. Worse than Darba Winters ever gets."

"You know that is not our way, Vesta. And I've warned your father that he'll be shunned."

Defiantly, Vesta stared back at the bishop as if he were foolish. "I can't live there anymore, Bischoff."

Gently, Cal asked Vesta, "Do you have a place to stay?"

"I'm going down to the jail, to talk with Crist."

"But do you have a place to stay tonight?" Cal asked.

Vesta turned to the pastor and considered her answer. "I could go to Sara Miller's place. In the Doughty Valley. She and Jeremiah were going to help Crist and me. So, I guess I could go there."

Cal asked, "Is this Jeremiah, the son of Jonah and the grandson of Eli?"

"Yes. They have the bishop's old house."

Cal nodded. "Do you want me to drive you there?"

Hesitating, Vesta said, "I've already got my horse and buggy here."

Bishop Shetler offered, "We can take it home for you, Vesta."

As Vesta considered this, the people standing together at the top of Darba's drive shifted about and made a path for Deputy Armbruster to pull his cruiser in beside the driveway. When the people all turned to look down the drive, Vesta cried out and ran forward, pushing through to the front of the group. Coming up the drive, they saw Sergeant Niell escorting Crist Burkholder, whose hands were cuffed in front.

Beside them walked Linda Hart, saying to Crist, "I'll follow you into town, Crist. Don't say anything. Don't talk to them at all. Do you understand?"

Crist nodded, head hanging down.

Vesta shouted, "Crist!" and ran down to meet them. She tried to reach out to Burkholder, but Niell waved her off and told Burkholder, "Keep moving."

Vesta back-stepped up the drive in front of them, pleading, "I need to talk to him. Just let me talk to him."

But Niell denied her, saying, "Maybe down at the jail," as he held a hand on top of Burkholder's head to guide him into the backseat of Armbruster's cruiser.

6

Wednesday, October 7
9:15 A.M.

WHEN ARMBRUSTER pulled his cruiser away, Vesta Miller collapsed in the gravel at the top of Darba's drive. Several of the women rushed to her and knelt beside her, rubbing her arms and shoulders, trying to calm her. But she lay stiffly on her side hugging her chest, muttering, "No, No, No," and nothing the women said to her brought a sensible response.

Eventually, they managed to prop her up into a sitting position, and she appeared to focus her sight on the barn. Then, looking from one person to another, she asked the women beside her, "What can I do? What can we do?"

Cal knelt beside Vesta, and the women stood to let him speak with her. On his knees, he said, "Go home with Katie. Go to the bishop's house and try to rest."

"No, No, No," Vesta cried. "I want to talk to Crist."

Cal said, "You can see him later, Vesta. At the jail. I'll drive you down, but first, go to Katie's. Sit a bit. Take some food. Then, I'll come get you, and we'll drive into town."

Trying to stand, Vesta was still unsteady. "I need to talk to him now."

Cal helped her to her feet and supported her elbow. "Let Katie help you, first. You don't look so good."

One of the other women stepped forward and said to Cal, "My place is closer, Pastor. Let me take her. We're just up the road. The next farm."

"OK," Vesta whispered.

Cal handed her to the woman and said, "I'll come for her

this afternoon. Crist won't be able to talk much before then, anyway. But get her to lie down. Maybe eat something."

The woman nodded, and with help from two others, she guided Vesta toward her buggy.

* * *

The rest of the crowd seemed to be dispersing. At the edge of Darba's front lawn, Cal saw Leon and Katie Shetler talking with the Burkholders. He joined them and said to Wayne Burkholder, "I'll take Vesta into town a little later, but maybe you two should go into Millersburg to see about Crist, now."

Wayne Burkholder nodded. "That's what we were talking about. But we don't know if the sheriff will let us talk to him."

"He will," Cal assured them. "Eventually. In the meantime, the best thing is to be there when they're ready. You'll want to speak to his lawyer, too. Linda Hart. Maybe you should do that first."

Wayne nodded, and looked to Bishop Shetler and then back to Cal. Then he nodded again and with clarity of purpose, he hurried with his wife Mary toward their buggy.

To the bishop, Cal said, "Leon, I think you've got some mending to do in Jacob Miller's family."

"I didn't know it was so bad," Shetler said.

"Can you find Jacob Miller?" Cal asked. "Take him aside?"

Shetler shook his head sadly. "I'll want to speak with his wife, Cal. I should do that first. Besides, I just spoke with Jacob."

"OK," Cal said, eyeing the picture window at the front of the Winters house. Darba stood there gazing out at them with the transfixed expression of someone asleep on her feet. "Maybe someone needs to check on Darba, too," Cal remarked.

Katie and the bishop turned to look back at Darba, and Katie said, "I can do that."

"She might not let you in," said Cal.

"Maybe if I asked to use her bathroom," Katie said. "That sometimes gets me in. She doesn't feel so much like I'm just checking on her."

Cal agreed. "I was out here last week, and she wouldn't let me through the door. She would barely talk through the screen."

"It's worse when Billy's gone," Katie observed. "He should be down in Pinecraft today, so that's going to be a problem for her."

"Maybe we should call Evie Carson," Cal said.

"Maybe Darba already has done that," Leon suggested.

"But you'll try?" Cal asked Katie. "Try to check on her?"

"Of course."

"She might be into her 'negativities.'"

"I can try," Katie said. "Can't hurt."

"OK," Cal said. "I'll be up in a bit. First, I want to talk to the sheriff, down at the barn."

The bishop touched Cal's arm. "Who else, Cal? Who else do we need to worry about?"

Cal thought through the list. Darba, Vesta, Crist, the Burkholders, the family of Jacob Miller. Then he asked, "Was anyone particularly close to Glenn Spiegle?"

"Billy Winters was his closest friend. They knew each other in Florida, before Billy moved up here."

"But is there anyone in your district, Leon?"

"None more than another," Leon replied. "The people were slow to accept him."

Cal asked, "But was anyone helping him? Or spending time at his place?"

"I guess that'd be me," Shetler replied.

"And are you OK, Leon?" Cal asked.

Shetler thought, looked to Katie and back to Cal. "I think I'm numb, Cal. You know, shocked."

"Can you find a phone from time to time?"

"Why?"

"Because if I don't get back out here, you could call. We could talk."

Shetler tilted his head, thinking ruefully of the irony built into Cal's suggestion. Thinking of the first time he had used a phone—that morning in Mony Detweiler's maple grove. "I guess I could find a phone from time to time."

* * *

The coroner's wagon was parked at the bottom of the drive, backed up to the large barn doors, and as Cal came down the slope, two of Missy's assistants were pulling a gurney out of the back. Cal stepped around them and entered the barn.

Missy's floodlights had been switched off and packed into their canvas cases, but the murder scene was now well lit by sunlight coming through the large openings of the barn doors. The back of the barn was in shadow, but a light was on in the Rumspringe Room, and Bruce Robertson stood just inside the room's single door, talking with Missy. Cal stepped past the body of Glenn Spiegle, which was still covered with a tarp, and went back to talk with the sheriff and the coroner.

When he entered the Rumspringe Room, Missy was saying to her husband, "Bruce, he told Ricky that he didn't move the body."

Robertson turned his attention to Cal and, sweeping his arm around the room, he asked, "What do you make of this?"

Not bothering to inspect the room, Cal said, "It's a Rum Room, Bruce. Darba lets the Amish teenagers use it."

"You're not surprised?" Robertson asked.

"I've spent some time with Darba," Cal said. "Her intentions are good."

Missy argued, "But Cal, she's got a whole apartment here. Everything except a bed."

Cal glanced around and shrugged, "It's a safe place for the kids."

Robertson asked, "Does the bishop know about this?"

"I'm sure he does."

"You don't think this is strange?" Missy asked.

Considerably taller than Troyer, Missy was almost her husband's height. But unlike the heavy sheriff, Missy was not overweight. Neither was she thin or frail. She had taken her examiner's cap off, and the waves of her brown hair were tied back in a long ponytail. Her white lab coat was folded on her arm. Again she asked, "Not even a little bit strange, Cal?"

Cal shrugged. "Darba's got a heart for the kids. She used to be a teacher."

Coarsely, Robertson remarked, "Yeah, Cal, and they kicked her out of that job."

"She has some problems," Cal allowed. "But Darba was one of the best teachers we ever had out here."

Robertson snorted. "Cal! She's letting Amish kids run wild in her barn!"

"Kids are kids," Cal said. "They need a safe place to go, and Darba's generosity is well intentioned. She does good here."

"That's just great!" Robertson shot. "She's giving them an excuse to run loose."

"You want them running loose in town?"

"I don't want them running loose at all," Robertson said.

"Yeah, well, that's not likely."

Robertson gave up, said, "I've got to get going," and walked out into the open barn. Cal followed and said to the sheriff's back, "The Burkholders are going to want to talk to Crist. Vesta Miller, too."

The sheriff kept going and talked back over his shoulder. "He's got to be processed first. You know that."

Cal advanced and pulled at the sheriff's arm to turn him back around. "But this afternoon, Bruce, I'll bring Vesta down."

"Whatever."

"Bruce, this needs to be handled gently. The Amish don't know anything about criminal matters."

Robertson considered the pastor's intensity and softened. "I'll let them talk to him as soon as his lawyer says it's OK."

7

Wednesday, October 7
MORNING

FEELING STIFF and mechanical, but trusting that Dr. Carson had been right on the phone, Darba went slowly about the business of the normal, getting herself out of her bathrobe and into something "comfortable and happy," as Carson had put it—a loose-fitting sundress with a purple and green trillium pattern. She pulled the dress over a white cotton blouse and slipped into a pair of summer sandals, starting to remember some of the details about finding the body and calling 911.

In jerky, awkward sequences, as if it were an old, silent movie in her mind, she saw herself walking up to the body of Glenn Spiegle, sprawled out prone on the concrete, beside the blue Chevy.

A sad *Oh, Billy!* sparked in her thoughts. *Your best friend. Murdered while you are in Florida.*

An Amish lad had admitted doing it? Was that possible? But she had seen him running up her drive. It was his car she had found running in the barn.

Then the bullish sheriff had come—crawling through her barn. Nosing into her Rum Room, no doubt. And Oh! How much they would judge her for keeping that room! "Crazy Darba" is what they'd all say, Amish and English alike.

But her medicine was starting to help now, and instead of nursing her "negativities" as she sometimes was inclined to do, Darba knew to stand at the picture window and wait for Dr. Carson. "I'll be there as soon as I can," Carson had promised.

So, just stand here quietly, Darba told herself. Let the medicine work. Watch the people.

Bishop Shetler, out front. Katie, too.

Cal Troyer, up and down the drive.

Oh, Billy! her thoughts cried anew, as she swung back into a memory of the morning. *Do you know your friend is dead? Did you feel him go?*

Glenn Spiegle had tried so hard. He had tried so hard for a new life. Who will stand up for him now, Billy? You did everything you could, but who will stand up for him now?

Not the bullish sheriff, Billy. He never liked you, anyway. He doesn't know how much you did to help Glenn Spiegle. He doesn't know the real you. So, he won't stand up for Glenn. Not like you would.

How did Spiegle's troubles find him, all the way up here? He had made such a good start here with the Amish. But that's all gone now, Darba girl. That's all gone like your job.

Sadly shaking her head, and aware only intermittently of her thoughts, Darba found herself gazing out at her Amish neighbors and friends, gathered on her front lawn.

She knew them all, young and old. Children, parents, and grandparents. The younger parents had been students in her last sixth-grade classroom. Not so long ago, Darba girl. Grown now, with children of their own.

There's Ricky Niell, putting young Burkholder in the back of that cruiser. The cruiser driving away. People heading home.

Cal Troyer, with Leon, and Katie Shetler, watching her from her front lawn. Talking. Probably talking about you, Darba girl.

People out here won't let me teach anymore.

After a black spell, Darba thought again of the barn. *I didn't go to the barn right away. They'll never understand that. How my brain is slow to focus when I'm off my medicine. They don't understand how the smoke can drift into my mind. They never get the "tickle knees." Never get the "crinklies" inside their ears. So, they won't understand why I waited to go down to the barn.*

Never mind. Doesn't matter.

Glenn Spiegle tried so hard.

Oh, Billy! Billy. Your friend is dead. Why can't you answer your phone? Just switch it on for once. Just check your messages. The government can't always want to track you.

* * *

When Katie Shetler knocked on her front door, the smoke had been drifting again through Darba Winters's mind. She opened her eyes and stepped woodenly to the door. When she opened it, Katie spoke through the screen. "Darba, are you OK?"

Darba gave a halfhearted smile, and Katie pulled the screened door open. "Darba, can I use your bathroom?"

Darba nodded and stepped back. Katie stepped inside and said, "Can we make some coffee?"

To clear her thoughts, Darba stretched her eyes open wide and rolled her head from side to side.

"Make some coffee?" Katie asked again.

Darba studied Katie in the vestibule and settled her sight on Katie's Amish attire. *You have always rather liked it, Darba girl.*

An ankle-length dark plum dress, with four pleats in front, and four matching pleats in back. Tied at the waist with a plain and thin dark plum string. Plain, round neckline with a thin, stitched border. Covered in front with a white day apron. The fabric of Katie's sleeves gathered over the rounds of her shoulders. Over her hair bun, a white prayer cap, cloth ties hanging down over the back of her shoulders. On her feet, Katie wore plain black Rockport walkers, with about an inch of black hose showing at her ankles. Yes, Darba rather liked Amish attire.

Seeing Darba's thoughts drift away, Katie tried again. "Darba, let's put up some coffee. We can talk."

"Is someone looking after Vesta Miller?" Darba asked, turning slowly for the kitchen.

"Yes, Darba."

Darba stopped in the living room and turned back to Katie. "Her father is a monster."

"We can talk in the kitchen," Katie said, waving Darba on.

Darba started again toward the kitchen, and then she stopped again. "Who is helping Vesta?"

"She's next door, Darba," Katie said and led into the kitchen. "She's with Emma Peachey. I think Anna Mast is there, too."

In the kitchen, Katie took out Darba's coffee carafe and filled it with water at the sink. Darba stood haplessly in the doorway, watching Katie make the coffee. When the coffeemaker was chirping, Katie took a seat at Darba's kitchen table and waved for Darba to join her. Darba sat down and stared at the red Formica tabletop. After another slow roll of her head, she asked, "Are they upset with me for not going down to the barn right away?"

"I don't think so," Katie said. "I don't see why they would be."

Darba closed her eyes on a memory. "Glenn Spiegle didn't deserve to be beaten like that."

Katie glanced over at the coffeemaker and said, "I'm sorry you had to see that, Darba."

Eyes open again, Darba asked, "Did young Burkholder really say he did it?"

"He wouldn't lie, Darba."

"No, I suppose not."

When the pot had finished brewing, Katie got up, poured two cups, and brought them back to the table, saying, "Drink some coffee, Darba. It'll help if we talk."

"OK," Darba said and stared at the cup in front of her.

"Is Evie coming out?" Katie asked.

"I called her."

"Is she coming out this morning?"

"As soon as she can get here."

"We can talk while we wait."

"OK."

"Tell me what you're thinking."

"Smoke in my thoughts."

"Anything else?"

Darba shrugged. "It's a shame about Vesta. Her father is such a know-it-all."

8

Wednesday, October 7
10:30 A.M.

AS HE came up the Millers' long dirt drive in his buggy, Bishop Shetler met Jacob Miller walking out toward the blacktopped road, Township Lane 569, which makes a T-intersection with 601 about a mile north of the bishop's farm. Miller was carrying an old brown hard-shell suitcase, and he seemed to be in a hurry.

Shetler stopped his buggy on the drive and waited for Miller to come forward. Stopping beside Shetler's rig, Miller glanced anxiously down the drive to 569, and began to offer an explanation, saying, "Bischoff, I've got to take a short trip. I need to catch a taxi."

"You have a taxi coming to your house?"

"Well, one of the travel vans, really. I need to catch it at the end of the drive, there."

"Will you be gone long?"

"A few days. Maybe three or four."

"And your family?"

"They know their chores."

"Aren't you going to check on Vesta? She's still at the Peacheys' house."

"My Annie can check, Bischoff. I told her to check."

"You seem anxious, Jacob."

"I just need to catch this taxi."

"Where are you going?"

"Sarasota."

"Pinecraft?"

"Yes. Pinecraft."

"I didn't know a bus was leaving today."

Miller set his suitcase on the drive and took a handkerchief out of the side pocket of his britches. Despite the autumn coolness, his blue shirt was stained with sweat under his arms. He wiped his beaded brow, pushed the handkerchief back into his side pocket, and picked his suitcase up again, saying, "I'm not really taking a bus, Bischoff."

"You'd hire a taxi to go to Florida?"

Uneasy, Miller answered, "No, Bischoff, I am taking an airplane."

"We use vans and buses, Jacob. Not airplanes."

"It has to be a quick trip, Bischoff. The corn needs to come in next week, and I should be here for that, don't you think?"

"Yes," the bishop intoned. "You need to be here, with your family."

"I'll be back in a few days, Bischoff. We can talk then, if you wish."

Shetler looked down to the Miller house at the end of the long drive. A daughter was cutting grass with an old, smoky gasoline mower. Another daughter was hanging laundry out to dry on a line at the side of the house. The oldest son, Andy, stepped down from the front porch, waved to the bishop, and went into the barn to the right of the house. From the chimney of the grandparents' Daadihaus to the left, a thin line of gray smoke rose into the sky and blew away on a high breeze. The pinging of a hammer on metal came from an outbuilding beyond the barn, and at the front parlor window, the bishop could see a young girl gazing out between the long purple curtains.

No longer surprised by anything new he discovered about Jacob Miller, the bishop still considered it a revelation that Miller would be leaving town while his family was, from all reports, in such obvious crisis, and with his daughter Vesta struck numb by heartache and despair over Crist Burkholder. So he focused his stern attentions back on Miller and said, "Jacob, we are commanded to be 'as wise as serpents and as harmless as doves.' Do you still know what that means? I have preached about it many times at Sunday meetings."

Surprised and very much chastened by the bishop's tone, Miller nodded.

"Because, Jacob, I'm not sure, anymore, that you do understand this scripture."

Miller stared back in silent shock.

"Which of these two injunctions is written, Jacob, for the well-being of wolves?"

"What?"

"The verse begins, 'Behold I send you out as sheep among wolves. Wherefore be ye as wise as serpents and as harmless as doves.' So, I ask you, which of these two injunctions is written for the benefit of the wolves?"

After a long pause, Miller replied, "Bischoff, if you don't mind, I really do need to catch a ride. Can we talk when I get back?"

"The answer is 'Neither,' Jacob."

"What?"

"The answer to my question is 'Neither.'"

"What?"

Weary to the core, the bishop sighed out the full weight of his years, disinclined to explain his point further. "Then go along, Jacob," he said. "But when you fly home, come first to my house, not here to yours."

"Why, Bischoff?"

"I've got a decision to make about you, Jacob, but first I need to minister to your family."

"A decision?"

"Yes. Do you understand? Come first to my house, not to yours."

"I really don't understand, Bischoff."

"I know you don't, Jacob. Believe me, I know."

Miller shook his head as if he were perplexed by a great mystery, and Shetler stared back at him with calm certainty.

"Do you pray for your wife, Jacob?"

"Yes, Bischoff."

"What do you pray, Jacob?"

"That she will be steadfast, diligent, industrious."

"These are qualities in a wife that would please you, Jacob?"

"Yes."

Gazing sternly into Miller's eyes, the bishop asked, "What blessings do you pray for your wife, Jacob?"

Again Miller answered, "Steadfastness, diligence, industry, Bischoff. Are these not the qualities of a good wife?"

Shetler sighed with weariness and shame. He looked to his feet and said humbly and meekly, as if he were handing a jewel of great worth to a man who could not appreciate its value, "When she falls asleep in my arms, Jacob, in my prayers, I take Katie's name into the throne room of God, and I weep at His feet to thank Him for the joy she has brought to me. I weep at His feet to praise Him for His gift of her to me."

"Bischoff?" Miller asked, dumbfounded by the man's self-effacing sincerity.

Shetler let a long, disquieting moment pass while Miller grew ever more uncomfortable, and then he said, "Jacob, I am not going to let you go home to your family, until you have learned to pray for your wife."

9

Wednesday, October 7
10:45 A.M.

WHILE BRUCE and Missy were finishing their work in the barn, Cal knocked at Darba's back door. Katie Shetler opened the kitchen door and stepped out onto the screened porch to let Cal in. Darba was still seated at the kitchen table, nursing her first cup of coffee. She did not make an effort to greet Cal, other than to toe a chair out for him and nod that he should take a seat opposite her. Before she reclaimed her seat next to Darba, Katie poured Cal a cup of coffee and set it in front of him.

Once seated, Katie said to Cal, "Billy is in Florida."

"Won't answer his phone," Darba said to her coffee cup. "He doesn't know his friend is dead."

"Have you left messages?" Cal asked.

"About a hundred," Darba said. She looked over to encourage Katie to explain.

Katie said, "Billy doesn't like to leave his phone on. So, at the end of the day, he switches on only long enough to check his messages. Then, if he needs to call Darba, he uses a land line."

"He conserves his minutes?" Cal asked.

"No," Darba laughed. "He doesn't want the government to be able to track him."

"Does he take the battery out?" Cal asked. "Because they can still tell where the phone is, if he doesn't do that."

Darba smiled as if the question were sophomoric. "Of course, Cal. Billy likes to be thorough."

"He doesn't like the government?" Cal asked.

"Ha!" shot Darba.

"That'd be an understatement," Katie answered.

Cal smiled and tasted the coffee. Burnt, he thought. Need to make another pot.

"Darba," Katie asked, "have you ever told Cal what Billy does after he makes his deliveries?"

Cal shook his head as Darba told Katie, "No."

Then to Cal, Darba said, "He parks at Bradenton Beach to watch the sunsets. He won't switch on to check his messages until it's dark."

"But you said you left him messages this morning," Cal said. "Why would you do that, if you know he doesn't use his phone until after dark?"

"Got worried," Darba explained. "Maybe he'll check early, for once."

The doorbell rang, and Katie got up and started toward the living room to answer it. But before she reached the living room, Evelyn Carson pushed in and entered at the front door. She started through the living room, calling out to Katie, "Is she OK?"

"I can hear you, Dr. Carson," Darba sang out. "I'm fine."

Silently, Katie shook her head for Carson, who came through the living room and into the kitchen ahead of Katie. Taking the fourth chair, opposite Katie's cup of coffee, Carson sat down and studied Darba's eyes.

"Have you taken all of your medicine?" she asked Darba, and accepted a cup of coffee from Katie. Ignoring the coffee in front of her, Carson held her gaze on Darba and reached for her wrist to take her pulse. Familiar with the routine, Darba held her wrist out and said, "I'm much better, Dr. Carson. Finding the body threw me off. Forgot my morning meds."

Carson released Darba's wrist and nodded satisfaction. "I want you to tell me about your mood, Darba."

Darba glanced with embarrassment at Cal and then Katie, and Cal stood up, saying, "I'll clear out, so you two can talk."

Still standing, Katie said, "I'll check on the bishop. He said he'd need help at the Jacob Millers."

* * *

When they had left, Dr. Carson moved Darba into the living room and asked her to lie back in an easy chair and close her eyes. When Darba was positioned, Carson said, "First words, Darba. What are they?"

"Billy. Heartache. Spiegle. Beaten. Burkholder. Vesta. Vesta." She opened her eyes. "What will become of Crist and Vesta?"

That's rational, Carson thought, a good sign. "*Billy* was your first word, Darba. Why?"

Darba shrugged. "Glenn Spiegle was his best friend. They've known each other since they were kids. They grew up together, in Bradenton."

"I know Billy was trying to help him," Carson led.

"He did. He helped him start new, up here. After Glenn got out of prison."

"Why here, Darba? Why'd Spiegle come up to Ohio?"

"Billy was here, and they had a secret, Dr. Carson. He and Billy had a big secret."

"How long was Spiegle in prison?"

"I don't know for sure. Twenty years?"

"Darba, I want you to think about this. Why did you say 'Billy' first?"

Darba's eyes danced with anxiety, and she blurted out, "He has to run!"

"Because of something they did?"

Darba nodded. "It was Glenn Spiegle. It's why he went to prison."

"Billy was there, when Spiegle did something?"

Another nod, and Darba said, "They drank a lot back then."

"Billy's been sober for a long time," Carson said, intending encouragement. "He has you to thank for that."

"I know. He dried Glenn out, too. While Glenn was still in prison."

"How could he drink in prison?"

"Oh, you can get a lot of things in prison, Dr. Carson. And alcohol isn't the only thing that will get you high."

"Spiegle was using drugs?"

Darba nodded. "But he quit. Billy helped him, like I helped Billy."

"Again, Darba, why did you say *Billy* first, when I asked you for your first words?"

"Because he doesn't know Glenn is dead, Dr. Carson. He doesn't know to run."

10

Wednesday, October 7
11:55 A.M.

DR. CARSON asked Darba to lie down in her bedroom and gave her a sleeping aid, hoping that Darba could rest for a few hours. She promised Darba that when she woke up, they would talk some more about how to reach Billy before nightfall. She also promised that she would stay in the house while Darba slept.

While cleaning up coffee cups at the kitchen sink, Carson heard a knock at the back screened porch, and she went, towel in hand, to answer it.

Bruce Robertson was standing at the back door, peering in through the screen. Carson went out to him, opened the porch door, and stepped back to admit him. Down at the barn, she could see Deputy Pat Lance and Coroner Missy Taggert-Robertson fixing yellow crime scene tape over the big barn doors, which had been pulled closed and bolted in place.

Evelyn Carson was a short, round woman with blond hair clipped to an easy, wash-and-go style. Her features were continental—middle European, Robertson had always thought, with perhaps a hint of stubborn peasant stock in her attitude. She always stood her ground in front of the sheriff, as if she were defending the innocent against marauders, and today she blocked Robertson's way into Darba's house by standing in front of the sliding doors into the kitchen with her arms crossed over her chest, saying, "She's sleeping, Bruce. I don't want to wake her up."

Robertson shook his head. "I need to ask her again about this morning—when she says she found the body."

"What do you mean, 'says she found the body'?"

"So far, Evie, we've got only a partial account from Crist Burkholder. I need to hear what Darba found when she first went down to the barn."

"I can't let you do that, Sheriff. She needs to rest. You're just going to have to wait."

"I need to know if she saw the fight, Evie."

"More likely, you don't believe everything Crist Burkholder has told you, and you're just fishing."

Robertson complained, "I just need to know if she saw the fight."

"What makes you think she did?"

"Something she said when she called us."

"What?" Carson asked, impatiently.

Sighing, the sheriff said, "She *said* she didn't think an Amish kid could throw a punch like that."

"Maybe she got that from seeing Spiegle. You know, seeing the condition of the body."

"What do you know about that?"

Exasperated, Carson answered, "Nothing, Bruce."

"Sounds like you do."

"Well, I don't," Carson said, planting herself more firmly in the doorway.

"Did she tell you something?"

"No."

"Did she move the body?"

"I don't know."

"I need to ask her about these types of things, Evie."

"She's taken some medication. Might sleep for a couple of hours, if she's lucky."

Robertson studied Carson, thought, and said, "Is there something wrong with her? You know, aside from the usual?"

"Like what, Bruce?"

"Oh, I don't know, Evie. Maybe she saw the fight, and she's flipped out about it. That's why I need to talk with her."

Carson cracked a knowing smile. "I know how you operate, Bruce. You've handled some of my patients before."

Robertson studied the back windows of the house. "What's wrong, Doctor? Where's Billy?"

"He delivers cheese every week to Florida. He's down at the Pinecraft community."

Robertson took a step forward. "I want you to wake her up, Evie. Let me ask her some questions. Right here, today."

"I'm not going to do that, Sheriff. Now, stop wasting my time."

Pulling a grin for show, Robertson said, "Then I want you to bring her down to my office. When you think she can talk."

"Maybe tomorrow," Carson offered.

Robertson nodded and backed up to the porch door. "And I want to see Billy, too. As soon as he gets back."

"You can find Billy yourself, Sheriff. I'm not his doctor."

"But you'll bring Darba in?"

"When it's in her best interests."

"Of course, Evie, whatever."

"And Bruce?"

"What?" Robertson asked, impatient to leave.

"Don't call me *Evie.*"

"Carson, we've all called you *Evie* since the playgrounds at school."

"You're the sheriff now, Bruce, and I'm not that scrawny girl with pigtails anymore."

Robertson considered the doctor's expression and smiled. "Is it like that now, Dr. Carson?"

"Yes," Carson said. "As long as you're the sheriff, wanting to question one of my patients."

11

Wednesday, October 7
12:25 P.M.

BRUCE ROBERTSON stood at Courthouse Square in Millersburg and studied his old red brick jail with an attenuated degree of satisfaction, tainted with unease by the arrest he had made that morning at Darba Winters's barn. Amish as murderers? Robertson didn't like that notion at all.

But Burkholder's confession was solid. He had insisted more than once that he had killed Glenn Spiegle. And normally, Robertson wouldn't have hesitated to file charges. But an Amish murderer? That had to be wrong. So, standing outside the courthouse in bright afternoon sun, Robertson eyed the square exterior of his red brick jail and tried to draw reassurance from the way its old-fashioned solidity anchored its corner of the square.

The jail's two stories of Victorian brick and ornate yellow sandstone trim were topped with a black roofline sporting seven weathered chimneys and a tangle of satellite dishes, microwave arrays, and radio antennas. Its matching red brick extension on the back had eight large windows to a side, each covered on the exterior with a grillwork of black iron jailhouse bars.

It was not a modern structure by any means, and Robertson liked it that way. It looked old, it was old, and it promised to do its duty the old way—steadfastly, resolutely, and without compromise with the pop psychology that taught citizens that criminals were only human, after all. Maybe they were human, Robertson was fond of saying, but in his jail, they were first and last prisoners who owed society a debt for their lawlessness. That's how he saw it, and to his way of thinking, that's why he had been elected sheriff of Holmes County for thirty continuous years.

Bruce Robertson was the old, steadfast, resolute kind of sheriff, and that's just how Holmes County liked it. But Amish as murderers? At the very core of Robertson's steadfast resolve, that just didn't make sense. So, as he climbed the stone steps that took him to the north entrance of the jail, he drew scant satisfaction from the arrest. Crist Burkholder might have confessed, but Cal Troyer was right. This had to be handled differently. If Robertson were going to press forward, he'd first have to be convinced that the Burkholder confession could be trusted.

Inside, Robertson pushed through Ellie's swinging counter door and started down the long paneled hallway to his office, saying, "Coffee please, Ellie, and tell your layabout husband that I want to see him."

With a tap at her keyboard, Ellie saved a file on her computer, and said, "He's already in there."

Ellie followed the sheriff down the hall to Robertson's big corner office with a fresh tin of coffee. She nodded to Ricky, who sat in a straight-backed office chair in front of Robertson's cherry desk, and then she turned to the credenza behind the door and started to put up a fresh pot of coffee for the sheriff.

Robertson dropped into a battered swivel rocker behind his desk and asked Sergeant Niell, "Where'd you put him?"

"Second floor," Niell said. "Gave him his own cell."

Taking papers out of his in-box, Robertson asked, "He still in his Amish clothes?"

Niell answered, "Yes," and holding up a blue form, Robertson asked Ellie, "What's this?"

Ellie finished with the coffee pot, turned to look, and took a seat in a chair beside Ricky. "County's got a new Emergency Contacts form, Bruce. You're supposed to fill that out with all your numbers."

The sheriff rolled his eyes and crumpled the blue form into a tight ball before he launched it at his wastepaper basket. Ellie retrieved the crumpled blue form, saying, "We recycle now, Bruce."

Robertson smiled and continued to sort papers, some into his out-box, most back into his in-box. To Niell he said, "When did Ellie turn into a recycling enviro-nut, Sergeant?"

Ricky shrugged a halfhearted answer, hoping Ellie would let it drop. But seated at his side again, Ellie said, "I'm moving us into the digital world, Bruce. Then you won't get any more paper to waste."

Ellie's dark hair was styled long and straight, and her skirt and blouse outfit was plain and simple, soft green and rose colors typical of those favored by Mennonite women, although Ellie wasn't Mennonite. But with her hair in a bun under a white prayer cap, and wearing simple, black flats and black hose, she would easily pass for Mennonite anywhere in Holmes County. It wasn't a deception she tried to practice; she just preferred simple dresses and skirts at work. And when opportunities like this one presented themselves, she also preferred to pester the sheriff with her assertiveness. So she smiled and stated, "We're just gonna get modern."

"That's how it is?" Robertson grinned, leaning back on his swivel rocker, hands clasped behind his head.

"That's exactly how it is," Ellie said and smiled.

The coffeepot finished chattering, so Ellie got up to pour some coffee for the two men. At Robertson's door, Ellie said, "I put our new intake and discharge forms on our FTP server." Stepping out into the hall, she added, "That's not the kind of *server* you find at a restaurant, Bruce."

"Like I know how to use an FTP *server,*" Robertson complained to Niell once Ellie was gone.

Niell wanted to smile, but he couldn't decide if Robertson would interpret that kindly, so he shrugged and said, "I called that restaurant down in Pinecraft. They say Billy Winters delivered a truckload of Kline's Amish cheese this morning. They say he's already left."

Robertson nodded. "Probably no point in checking on him with the Klines. They'll confirm the shipment."

"It was a long shot, anyway," Niell said.

"No longer a shot than thinking that an Amish kid is guilty of homicide."

"I suppose not."

"OK, Ricky," Robertson said. "Let's write it up for the prosecutor, but hold the paperwork. I'm not ready to press forward, yet."

"What charge?"

"Manslaughter, for now. But don't file the charges, just yet."

"Let me interview him again," Ricky offered. "Maybe Spiegle provoked him."

"It'll still be manslaughter," Robertson said. "If he really did it."

"I'll just make sure."

Robertson shrugged a detached approval. "You think Ellie is serious about going all digital, here?"

"You should use her to get us modern, Sheriff. While she's still working."

"What's that mean?"

"She'd be an asset, if we all need to take it to the next level with IT."

"No. What's that mean—'while she's still working'?"

"We want to have a family."

"You think she'd stop working?"

"I know she would."

"What are you, Ricky? Thirty-five?"

"Thirty-eight."

"And Ellie?"

"Thirty-four."

Robertson considered that. "You'll make lieutenant by the time you're forty."

Smiling, Ricky said, "Sheriff, I'm really not sure I want to work for you for the rest of my life."

There was a knock through the wall, and they heard Ellie sing out, "You have *company*, Bruce!"

Robertson pushed up from his chair and started out to the front just as Cal Troyer opened the door to the office and came in, announcing, "Bruce, I want to talk with Crist Burkholder."

"Cal, you need to let us handle this," Robertson complained, and dropped back into his swivel chair.

Cal nodded to Ricky, "Sergeant," and took a seat next to him in front of the sheriff's desk. "Bruce, you need to move him to a single cell. He shouldn't be in with the others."

Ricky said, "We already did that."

Cal nodded his appreciation to Niell and said, "Rachel says you helped her out, a couple of days ago."

"Out at Kline's," Ricky said. "There were too many kids skateboarding on the parking lot."

"She's a technician there," Cal said for Robertson's benefit. "She handles their Information Technology Services. You know, Bruce, IT."

Robertson quipped, "Like a cheese factory needs IT," and pulled papers out of his in-box again.

"You need to get a little modern yourself, Bruce," Cal chided. "Nobody uses *in and out* trays anymore."

Growling, Robertson said, "You two can have your reunion out in the hall," and stood up behind his desk.

Cal shrugged at the sheriff's gruff tone, smiled his awareness of Robertson's impatience, and followed the sergeant out into the hall, saying, "I need to talk to Crist, Ricky. Can you take me up?"

Ricky paused outside Robertson's door and said, "He claims he did it, Cal. Burkholder says he hit him."

Cal started toward the stairwell at the end of the hall, saying, "I know, Ricky. I just want to talk to him about court practices."

"Why?" Ricky asked, following Cal down the hall.

Cal answered, "Amish folk don't know anything about trials."

"There probably won't be a trial, Cal."

"Won't he have to explain himself to a judge?" Cal asked.

"Sure. If the judge requires it. He'll have to admit to what he did."

Cal nodded and started up the steps. "I doubt he knows what that means."

"He's gonna have a lawyer, Cal," Ricky argued.

"Let me talk to him, Ricky. I'll just be a minute."

"Take all the time you want, Cal," Ricky said at the top of the steps. "He's not going anywhere."

* * *

When Ricky opened the cell door, Cal pulled a chair inside from the aisle between the cell blocks and sat down next to Burkholder. Crist was seated on the edge of his bunk, elbows planted on his knees, head cradled in his hands. He did not look up when Cal sat down.

Dressed in his Amish clothes—blue denim trousers and a blue cotton blouse, but without his black cloth suspenders—Burkholder looked as out of place as a peasant in Tiffany's. His brown leather work boots, hanging open as if they were three sizes too large, had been stripped of their shoelaces. A blue denim vest with hook and eye closures hung limp from his shoulders, open in front. His black hair was cut to the tops of his ears in Dutch-boy style, and his face and neck were tanned, his forehead showing pale white skin where his straw hat had shaded his eyes through the long summer in open fields. He had started a fancy beard, trimmed thin along the jawline, broadcasting his unmarried status and his spirited personality. But there in his cell, all of Crist Burkholder's spirit and personality had been quenched, and his fancy beard communicated more bravado than was warranted.

Cal reached up to lay a hand on Burkholder's broad shoulders, intending to minister comfort to the lad, but Burkholder pulled back sullenly.

Removing his hand, Cal said, "I arranged for you to have a lawyer, Crist. To help you navigate the courts."

"She's a woman," Burkholder said, and stood up to stare down dully at Cal. "I've already met my lawyer, and she's a woman."

"Is that going to be a problem?"

"Doesn't matter. I'm guilty."

"You still need to listen to her advice."

"She says I'm going to prison, if I confess in court."

"Look, Crist, if she says you shouldn't confess, then maybe you shouldn't."

"But I already did."

Standing, Cal offered, "Maybe she'll have a way to work around that."

"Doesn't matter. I did it. I killed him."

Cal studied Burkholder's expression for signs of contrition, but all he saw was the self-disgust of a boy who believed wholeheartedly that he was the author of his own disgrace. Thinking Burkholder should have been more concerned about his future, Cal asked, "What does your bishop say, Crist?"

Burkholder shook his head. "He says I have to take my medicine."

"Do you agree?" Cal asked.

"Sure. I did it. Now I'll die in prison."

"Crist," Cal asked, "did Glenn Spiegle provoke you?" and laid his hand back on Burkholder's shoulder.

Again Burkholder pulled away at Cal's touch.

"What's wrong, Crist? What haven't you told us?"

Burkholder offered nothing.

"You're upset," Cal said. "I don't blame you. I would be upset too, if I were sitting in a jail cell. But people want to help you now, and you need to let them do that."

"Why, Mr. Troyer? Why do I have to let anyone help me? I killed a man. I beat him to death with my fist. Now I deserve what I get."

"Do you believe that, Crist? That you deserve whatever punishment you get?"

"Yes!" Burkholder shouted. "I killed a man! Don't you understand?"

"OK, Crist, but let some of us try to help you."

Burkholder shook his head and turned to face into the corner of the cell. "Please leave me alone."

"I will," Cal said. "But listen, just this once."

"What?" Burkholder said, turning back toward Cal. "You think I don't deserve to go to prison?"

"Probably you do, Crist."

"What can anyone do for me now?" Burkholder asked, facing back into the corner like a chastened youngster.

Softly Cal said, "Maybe you can get out, someday."

Turning around again, Burkholder asked, "How?" eyes cast down with shame.

"I don't know. But maybe you don't need to go to prison for the rest of your life."

"I murdered a man," Burkholder said, turning his gaze up to Cal's.

"The law distinguishes between murder and manslaughter, Crist. And manslaughter is not as bad. Maybe you could think about the day when they'll let you out of prison."

"They'd do that?"

"Eventually, yes. But it depends, now, on what happens in court."

"What should I do?"

"For starters," Cal said, "stop telling people you killed him."

"That's all?"

"That's just for starters," Cal said and turned to knock on the cell door.

As Sergeant Niell opened the door from the outside, Cal added, "In the meantime, Crist, you need to listen to your lawyer."

"She's a woman."

"She's a very good lawyer, Crist. That's all you should care about."

12

Wednesday, October 7
1:45 P.M.

BACK ON the first floor of the jail, Cal knocked on Bruce Robertson's door and went inside to find the sheriff frustrated, clicking uselessly with his mouse, and mumbling as one document after another opened up on his monitor. The sheriff caught Cal smiling, and he shoved his mouse aside and barked, "I hate these stupid Internet servers!"

Cal asked, "May I?" and Bruce rolled his chair back to let Cal lean over in front of the monitor. Cal clicked through all fourteen of the documents the sheriff had managed to open, closing each one in turn, and got Robertson's computer back to the desktop presentation—a special little item that Ellie had rigged for the sheriff—lilies and lambs scattered over a field of robin's-egg blue.

"Cute, Bruce," Cal said when he discovered the desktop theme. "Now, what were you looking for?"

Robertson sighed, "New intake and discharge forms. Ellie said they're supposed to *be on the server.*"

Still leaning over in front of Robertson's computer, Cal clicked keys and the mouse, navigated to the department's FTP site, and pulled up a folder labeled "New Forms." This he dragged onto Robertson's desktop, and when he opened it, he found a document labeled "Booking Sheet." He highlighted the document, said, "It's right here," and opened it for the sheriff.

Robertson rolled his eyes and leaned as far back in his swivel rocker as he could manage, as if to say he couldn't sit far enough away from the machine.

Cal tapped the screen and asked, "That's what you're looking for?"

Robertson nodded and stared blankly at the monitor, hands clasped behind his head.

Cal shrugged a smile, stood up, and changed the subject. "Bruce, Crist Burkholder doesn't have the slightest idea how this is going to play out for him. Not the faintest idea how the courts work."

"He's got a lawyer," Robertson argued.

"He's Shetler Amish, Bruce," Cal countered. "That's Leon Shetler's group, and they haven't got any experience with the law."

"*That's why he's got a lawyer!*" Robertson sang, still frustrated by Ellie's push for digital modernization. Still frustrated by the new computer on the corner of his desk. Half a dozen times he had considered just shoving it off the edge onto the floor, and claiming it slipped.

Cal watched the sheriff churning unhappy thoughts and eventually said, "Ellie can help you with this, Bruce. She's bored, just handling your usual business."

"Oh, she is?"

"Frankly, yes. You should let her drag you into the twenty-first century. You'd be doing her a favor."

Robertson considered that angle, and Cal could tell from the sheriff's expression that he liked the way Cal had phrased it—"Doing her a favor." But Cal wasn't willing to let the sheriff settle on that one rather belittling aspect of the characterization, so he added, "Ellie's the most accomplished assistant you've ever had, Bruce. You've seriously underutilized her."

Robertson came forward on his chair, considered that, and decided he couldn't find a satisfactory way to scowl about it. He studied the flat, serious stare on the pastor's face, assessed that he was seeing forthright honesty rather than challenge, and he said, "Sure, Cal—computers. IT. Why not?"

Cal tipped his head and said, "Now let me tell you about Crist Burkholder."

Robertson leaned back on his rocker and waved the pastor ahead.

"Leon and Katie Shetler have fifteen children, all grown. He's the bishop out there. They are Old Order Amish to a point, but not conservative like some outfits. Certainly not like the Schwartzentrubers."

"Why do I care about this, Cal?"

"Bear with me, Sheriff. Now, Crist Burkholder is Leon's nephew. He's the son of Wayne and Mary Burkholder, and Mary is the sister of Leon's wife, Katie. She herself is the middle of thirteen children. The whole Shetler sect is spread out along Township 601, out on the ridge overlooking the valley at Leeper School, south of Fredericksburg. That's where Billy and Darba Winters live, right in the middle of the Shetler bunch, on a stretch of road with four other English families."

"Cal!" Robertson complained.

"No, Bruce. You need to get this."

The sheriff waved him ahead with a scowl.

"Leon and Katie Shetler have the farm on the highest ground out there. You can see three counties at once from their front porch. At night you can see the lights of cars on Rt. 83, heading into Millersburg. That's probably ten miles away."

Robertson raised his palms to say, "So what?"

Cal nodded. "That's an out-of-the-way corner of the county, Bruce. That's as far back, out of the way, as you can get. And as long as you've been sheriff, I'd bet you've never had any trouble from anyone out there."

"So?"

"So, now you've got the murder of an Amish man and a confession from an Amish fellow, and Bishop Shetler wasn't even sophisticated enough about legal matters to advise his nephew to wait to talk to a lawyer first."

"But Burkholder does have a lawyer—Linda Hart."

"I know, Bruce. I lined her up for him."

"I'd have gotten him court-appointed counsel, Cal. You know that."

"I got him someone better."

"Why?"

"That's what I'm trying to explain to you. As far as understanding the law is concerned, these are extremely backward people."

"OK, Cal, I get it. But even Linda Hart isn't going to be able to get this kid off."

"I don't expect she will."

"Then what are you doing?"

"Maybe she can get him a lighter sentence. Maybe get him a reduced charge. Maybe a chance for parole sometime before he's an old man."

Robertson showed the pastor no opinion in his expression, but inwardly he congratulated Cal for his kindness. "You going to pay for the lawyer, Cal?"

"She's doing it *pro bono,*" Cal said, stepping to the door. As he opened the door, Cal turned back and added, "I can show you how to navigate to your FTP server, Bruce."

"Don't need you to do that," Robertson muttered.

Cal thought, hesitated, and said, "Like I said, Bruce, my daughter is IT chief for the Klines. She could give you a lesson or two, on your computer."

Robertson ran his eyes up toward the ceiling to think, and then he looked sheepishly back at Cal and asked, "Would anyone have to know about that?"

* * *

As Cal was walking out of the jail, Linda Hart was coming up the steps to go in. She took him lightly by the elbow and led him down the short steps to stand on the lawn near the Civil War monument. There, Hart leaned down close to Cal and whispered, "You knew, didn't you, Cal. Or, if you didn't know, I'm betting that you guessed."

Hart was a tall, solid woman with large ears and a narrow face made angular by a long Roman nose. Her small mouth with straight, thin lips seemed humorless to those who didn't know her well, and her height and angularity were enhanced by the austere business suits she wore. Her commanding tone in the courtroom led most people to conclude that she was too aggressive to be polite or too intense to be pleasant.

"Knew what, precisely?" Cal asked Hart.

Still leaning over close to his ear, Hart whispered, "That the Burkholder confession is 'bent' somehow wrong, Cal. It's kinked funny. It bends where it shouldn't, and I can't put my finger on it."

Cal led Hart to one of the iron benches spaced along the sidewalk surrounding the courthouse square, and he sat with her by the street, where the noise of traffic would give them some cover for their voices. As a tour bus huffed by on the street in front of them, he asked Hart, "You don't believe his confession?"

"I do, but only to a point, Cal."

"Robertson says he confessed to him and to his bishop. More than once. And just between you and me, he told me the same thing."

"I know, Cal. I've already talked to him."

"So?"

"So, Burkholder says the same thing each time. To Robertson and to me. But it's bent strange, Cal. I can't put my finger on it, but it's not a straight deal. It's strange in some way that I can't figure out."

"Don't you think Bruce will have noticed the same thing, Linda?"

"Cal, of course not. Bruce Robertson is the kind of dope who'd use a chess set for a checker game."

"OK," Cal laughed. "Maybe he's not seeing it."

"I'm not really *seeing* it, either, Cal. I've just got a hint of something's being wrong."

"Kinked, you say?"

"Not straight. Not straightforward."

"I've got to tell you, Linda, I've heard him confess, too. And if Bruce files against him and Crist says anything like that in court, he's going to prison."

"I know," Hart smiled. "But oh, how I love this hunch. Bruce Robertson is going to take a two-foot ladder down a ten-foot well, and I'm just going to leave him there."

"But what are you really going to do?"

Lifting a small recorder out of her purse, Hart said, "I'm going back to talk with Crist again. I'm going to have him tell it to me a dozen times, if I have to."

Cal watched traffic roll by on the street, and said, "Do you think he's innocent?"

"I don't know, Cal, but his confession doesn't ring true to me."

"I'd be surprised if he were lying," Cal said, turning back to face Hart.

"I don't think he is. I just know I don't believe it. Not as far as it goes. I don't think he murdered anyone."

Distracted by new possibilities, Cal remarked, "I was headed over to church. I have to prepare for Wednesday night services."

"It's OK, Cal. I've got this."

"I'm going out to see Vesta Miller after dinner. Can I tell her anything?"

"I don't know, Cal. I only have hunches here. But I think I'm right, and you can tell that much to Vesta."

13

Wednesday, October 7
2:30 P.M.

IN CRIST Burkholder's jail cell, Linda Hart sat on the bunk and switched on her tape recorder. "Crist," she said, "I want you to tell me again what you did. I want you to tell me why you did it."

Burkholder studied the recorder in Hart's hand, and then he glanced at Hart briefly, stared at the floor, and asked, "Are there a lot of women lawyers?"

Hart switched off the recorder, and with a hint of an aggressive tone, said, "Is this going to be a problem for you, Crist? Because from where I sit, you need to be focused on the things that matter to your defense."

"Maybe it does matter, Ms. Hart."

"At least you're not calling me Mrs."

"What?"

"Doesn't matter. Look, Crist, I'm your lawyer. Why should it matter to you that I'm a woman?"

"It doesn't matter to *me*."

"Then to whom should it matter, Mr. Burkholder? Who gets hung up on this type of silliness, anymore?"

"It doesn't matter to me, Ms. Hart, but it would matter to certain men in my church. And if the judge or somebody important thinks like that, too, then it'll matter to my defense."

Impressed with the logic, Hart said, "I'm glad to see that you're finally interested in your defense."

"Mr. Troyer says I might get out of prison, someday."

Hart nodded. "I'm going to try to keep you out of prison altogether."

Burkholder smiled and glanced at Hart, this time for a little longer. "It's just that Vesta's father—and one or two other men in my church—don't think women should be in charge of things."

"Do *you* think that, Crist?"

"No. I wanted to get Vesta away from that. Her thinking is too modern for Amish ways. Mine, too. We were leaving."

Hart switched on her tape recorder. "Leaving town?"

"Leaving the church. We were supposed to elope this morning."

"You'd quit the church? Both of you?"

"No, but we were going to elope and find a Mennonite church. Stop living Amish."

"Did anyone know that, Crist?"

"Darba Winters. She knew. And I told Glenn Spiegle."

"When?"

"Right before I killed him."

"Why would you tell him anything, Crist?"

"He stopped me in the barn. We argued. And I told him he couldn't marry Vesta, because I was going to marry her this morning. I told him we were leaving."

"Were you on your way to get Vesta?"

Burkholder nodded. "The car was already running, and I was packing the trunk. He came in and started yelling at me. Said that he'd die if he couldn't marry Vesta."

"What did you say?"

"I told him Vesta couldn't live Amish anymore."

"Then what?"

"He tried to give me money, and that made me mad. So I threw it back at him, and he threw it into the trunk."

"Is that when you hit him?"

"Yes," Burkholder whispered, the shame of it registering in his features.

"Tell me everything that happened, then, Crist. Everything you can remember."

"He dropped straight down at the back of the Chevy. His legs were tangled underneath him."

"What next?"

"I felt his neck, like they do on the TV."

"You thought he was dead?"

"I'm sure he was. He sure looked dead."

"Did you move him?"

"I think I just ran away. That's all I remember—running up the driveway."

Hart switched her recorder off. "Crist, when they found Spiegle's body, he was laid out straight on his back. He'd been severely beaten, by someone who was very angry with him."

"Then I must have done that," Crist said, "and I don't remember it."

"Show me your hands, Crist."

Burkholder held out his palms.

"No, the other side. The knuckles."

Burkholder flipped his hands over. They were the large, meaty hands of a farmhand. Thick calluses, protruding knuckles, rough skin, cracked and jagged nails. And on none of his knuckles were there any cuts or bruises.

"Crist, did the sheriff let you clean up? Wash your hands? Anything like that?"

"No."

"Did you wash up earlier? Use any ointments?"

"I just ran right to the bishop's house."

Hart jammed her tape recorder into her purse and took out a point-and-shoot digital camera. She took several photos of Burkholder's knuckles and hands, with time stamps and a voice recording describing the shots as she took them. When she was finished, she packed the camera back into her purse and stood up.

Burkholder stood beside her and asked, "Glenn Spiegle was beaten pretty badly?"

Pensive, Hart answered, "Right."

"Why aren't my knuckles bruised?"

"I don't know. They should be."

Crist said, "The sheriff said I probably beat him, and I just don't remember it."

"I know," Hart said. "That's what I'd say, if I were the sheriff."

"Maybe that's what I did, then," Crist said. "I just didn't hurt myself very much. You know—tough skin, strong hands."

"You don't really believe that anymore, do you, Crist?"

"I don't know what to believe."

"Well, I do, Crist. And I know what to do about it, too."

"What?"

"Talk to the prosecutor."

"Is he a woman, too?"

Hart laughed and gave Burkholder a bear hug.

14

Wednesday, October 7
3:00 P.M.

ANNIE MILLER stood at her end of the long kitchen table with the coffeepot ready in her hand, in case the bishop asked for more. If it appeared he didn't like it, she was prepared to brew a fresh pot. Her daughter Anna Mae stood at the woodstove, prepared to cook whatever the bishop desired. Ham, bacon, eggs, fried mush, whatever he requested. Beef, pork, potatoes. Maybe a sandwich. Anna Mae was ready. She knew her duties well.

Both women stood motionless while the bishop took his first sips to test the brew. Too hot? Too cold? Annie worried that something would be wrong with it. So many times her Jacob had taught her that a woman couldn't be expected to be perfect, but one could always be expected to improve. Too cold? Warm it up, and next time be more attentive. Too hot? Have some cold water at hand. And, if a woman couldn't be expected to be perfect, she could at least be ready to compensate with a heart to serve. And if the brew wasn't proper, wasn't that an opportunity to learn? Yes, as her Jacob had said many times, she was lucky that he was so patient with her. And today, she hoped the bishop would be patient with her, too.

"Is it too hot, Bischoff?" she asked. "Or, should I warm it up?" Her heart really was prepared to serve. Her daughters were the same; the bishop would approve. They had all been taught well, too. Anyway, most all of them. All except maybe Vesta.

But of all the others, her Anna Mae was surely the best cook. She knew just how her father liked his breakfast bacon. She knew just how to cook his eggs. And he had praised her repeatedly for this skill. The other children had their special duties, too. Each one chosen and taught. The whole family working together. Not as individuals, but as a whole, a properly working body of the *whole.* They practiced the proper *oneness* of the family, with its head the father and husband, and all of it a reflection on him. Yes, Annie Miller and the children knew their places in the body of the family. Surely the bishop would see that. Surely he would approve.

"Anna Mae is such a fine cook, Bischoff," Annie said. "She'll make such a fine wife."

Leon Shetler sat at the head of the long plank table and knew that he was expected to admire the coffee. He could see plainly that Annie Miller was anxious to please him. But coffee really wasn't all that important to him. Fresh-brewed or instant, it didn't much matter to him. It was a good, hot drink on cold mornings, but instant coffee was all he bothered to make for himself.

But here, clearly, Annie Miller was anxious about her coffee. He was supposed to enjoy the afternoon cup she had served him. He'd drink some to be polite, but to him it was only a device to allow conversation. He'd drink a bit and try to talk to Annie. Yes, she was anxious about it, the bishop thought. Or was it more than that?

He glanced around the room, trying to see if there was another reason why the women were nervous. The red linoleum floor was waxed to a shiny brightness, and swept as clean as a dinner plate. The purple curtains in the window had recently been washed and pressed, and they hung straight and neat from their rods. The dishes were all put up in careful stacks on the open shelves, above spotless countertops. Even the hand towels, which should see everyday use, were hung neatly in place at the sink. No, the bishop thought, everything here is perfect. Perhaps too perfect.

And the girl Anna Mae, standing so still at the stove, made him nervous because she was so attentive. "Anna Mae," he said, "I'm fine. I'm really not hungry."

Stepping forward, Anna Mae asked, "Maybe some cheese, Bischoff? With tomato slices?"

"No, Anna Mae, thank you. Why don't you try to enjoy some of the afternoon, while I speak with your mother?"

Fingers knotting into her apron in front, Anna Mae glanced at her mother and turned earnestly back to the bishop. "I do have my chores, Bischoff, but I'll gladly prepare anything you might like."

"Just the coffee," Shetler said, raising his cup with a smile.

Anna Mae glanced again at her mother. Annie gave a nod, and the girl turned to leave.

Intending encouragement, Shetler said, "Thank you, Anna Mae," and with puzzlement showing on her face, Anna Mae left through the door to the back porch.

Annie Miller—wide at the hips and thick through her shoulders—stood at the far end of the table, wearing a plain navy blue dress with a white apron. Her black bonnet covered her ears and lay flat against her cheeks. Her plain white kitchen apron hung to full length in front, with black hose and shoes showing below the hem.

"Bischoff," she said, "Jacob is not home right now. Wouldn't you prefer to speak with him?"

"No, Annie," the bishop said. "Please sit down."

"Perhaps pie, Bischoff. I have ground cherry pie."

Allowing an edge of authority to sharpen his tone, Shetler said, "Please sit down, Annie." He knew he was regularly shown a degree of deference, because he served as bishop, but he judged that he was seeing something more troubling than simple deference in Annie's awkward response to him. "Please sit down," he said again. "We need to talk."

Hesitating, Annie said, "I am sorry about Vesta, Bischoff. Is this about her?"

Shetler shook his head. "I want to talk with you about Jacob."

Annie set the coffee pot on a trivet on the counter behind her, and took a seat opposite the bishop, at the far end of the table, saying, "Vesta is such a trial for Jacob, Bischoff. She tries his patience at every turn."

Shetler considered everything that had happened that day, and he judged that Vesta's being a "trial" for her father should have been the least of Annie Miller's concerns. He knew it was the least of his. "Annie," he said. "Do you know that Crist Burkholder and Vesta had made plans to elope?"

Nodding, she said, "But I didn't tell that to Jacob, Bischoff."

"You knew she was leaving?"

Another nod. "Vesta has her 'talks' with me. I don't tell Jacob, because it would only put him out of sorts."

"What does she tell you, Annie?"

Annie hesitated, so Shetler added, "I am your Bishop, Annie. I won't tell Jacob that we have talked, unless you want me to."

"You wouldn't tell him that we talked about Vesta, Bischoff?"

"No. Or that we talked about you."

Carefully, Annie led, "Vesta always has her 'talks' with me when Jacob is away."

"What do you talk about?"

"Oh, I just listen, Bischoff. I don't encourage this type of modern thinking."

"Does Vesta think her father is too stern?"

"Yes," Annie said, showing a degree of shame. "She says we women should be treated better. She says that we *are* better."

"Better than what?"

"Better than Jacob teaches, Bischoff."

"Is Jacob abusive, Annie? I am asking as your bishop."

"Vesta says he abuses his authority."

"Do *you* think he does that?"

"He is the husband, Bischoff. And the father."

"And?"

"Jacob says that the Bible teaches that he is the rightful head of the wife. The rightful head of the family."

Shetler sighed. "Does he *rule,* Annie, or does he *serve?*"

"Bischoff?"

"The Bible teaches the *service* of leadership, Annie, not the *hierarchy.*"

"Jacob teaches that a husband needs to rule as the head of his wife."

Shetler sighed and shook his head. "This is not what the Bible teaches, Annie. This is not the mature intent of the Word."

"Is the husband not the head?"

"Annie, please," Shetler said, pinching the bridge of his nose. "You have heard me preach about this many times."

Confused and near tears, Annie said, "I have tried so hard, Bischoff. I have tried so hard to serve him."

"I wish you had chosen a different word, Annie," the bishop said. "For Vesta's sake, I wish you had chosen a different word than *serve.*"

"Bischoff, I do not understand."

"I know," Shetler said, weary. "But I have told Jacob that I want to see him when he gets back. I want to see him at my house, before he comes home."

Tears fell, now, onto Annie's cheeks.

Gentle in his tone, because he wanted Annie to understand, Shetler said, "A lot is happening right now, Annie. Katie needs to help with Darba. Vesta is mending at the Peacheys'. Crist Burkholder is in jail, because Glenn Spiegle is dead. The sheriff's people are going through his house right now. And your husband is on an airplane to Florida. But when it has all been straightened out, Jacob is going to stay with me for several days."

"But, what about his family, Bischoff? What are we to do if he stays with you?"

Shetler ignored the question for the moment. "Has he gone to Pinecraft before, Annie?"

"Several times, Bischoff."

"How many, Annie?"

"Maybe five."

"Why does he go?"

"I don't know, really."

"Does he have family down there?"

"No."

Embarrassed for her, Shetler studied the backs of his hands. "Annie, until Jacob is allowed to come home, I want you to run the farm just as you would if he were here."

"Bischoff?"

"I want *you* to take charge, Annie. And run the farm. Bring in the feed corn. Raise your children. Keep the family."

Annie seemed confused, so he added, "After we get this all sorted out, I will send Katie to help you."

"Help me with what, Bischoff?"

Everything, the bishop thought. "Your family," the bishop said.

15

Wednesday, October 7
4:00 P.M.

AS THE afternoon sun cast shadows across the blacktop of 601, Bishop Shetler wheeled his buggy up the lane at Glenn Spiegle's house and found two sheriff's deputy's cruisers parked in front of the long porch. He parked off to the side, tied his buggy horse to a fence post, and mounted the steps to the front porch just as Stan Armbruster came out of the front door carrying an open crate of papers and books. On the top of the stack in the crate was Glenn Spiegle's Bible, an English/German side-by-side, which the bishop had given Spiegle on the day he was baptized into the church.

Armbruster stepped to the side to let the bishop come up the steps, and he said to Chief Deputy Dan Wilsher, "This is all there was, Chief."

Wilsher looked into the crate and said, "OK, it all goes in, Stan," and Armbruster carried the crate down to one of the cruisers.

Dan Wilsher was dressed in his usual plain gray business suit, with white shirt and red tie. His hair was gray, just long enough to be parted, and his gray eyes broadcast the pleasant features of down-home honesty. He carried more weight than his doctor thought ideal, but he was not overweight like the sheriff. He had come up through the ranks, starting young as a deputy out of college, and he was now Robertson's chief of deputies, happy to serve as number two in command, letting Robertson sweat out all the political dilemmas of elected office, while Wilsher handled the command details, supervising the day-to-day law enforcement routines for three duty shifts.

Bishop Shetler came up to the chief on the porch, offered his hand, and introduced himself. Then he glanced back at the deputy loading the crate into the trunk of his cruiser, and said, "Do you have to take everything? Even his Bible?"

"For the time being," Wilsher said. "His heirs can have it back, once this is settled."

"Sadly, Chief," Shetler said, "I am his only heir."

Wilsher framed a skeptical expression. "He doesn't have any family?"

"Only his church," Shetler said.

Wilsher nodded. "I understand he came up here from Florida."

"Yes. Two years ago."

"And he had no one down there?"

"No. His mother died several years ago. She was his last relative."

Wilsher studied the short Amishman and wondered how much Shetler knew about Spiegle's Florida past. "Bishop, can you walk through the house with me?"

"Not much to see," Shetler said.

"I know," Wilsher said, leading through the front door. "That's what surprises me."

In the front hallway, there was no entryway furniture. The hallway walls were painted flat white, like the ceiling, and the red cherry trim was of plain, bare wood, not yet stained or varnished. The wide floorboards were painted flat gray. At the front end of the hall, there were doorways to a small parlor to the left and a living room to the right, each room bare and unfurnished, with no lamps, no wall adornments, and no curtains.

Wilsher pointed out the two rooms and said, "He didn't really have much furniture, Bishop."

"No," Shetler said. "Not yet, anyway."

Farther down the hall, there was a staircase leading up to the second floor, and as he passed it, Wilsher said, "Only one of the bedrooms upstairs has any furniture."

The bishop nodded as he followed. “He had no family, Chief Deputy. That was all to come, later.”

In the kitchen at the back end of the hallway, Wilsher said, “This is all new, but it’s all old-fashioned.”

“Sure. You’d expect that,” Shetler said. “I helped him buy it all. At Lehman’s, in Kidron.”

Along one wall, Spiegle had an iron wood-fired cooking stove, with shiny silver metal features and black, cast-iron trim. Beside the stove stood a wooden chopping-block table with several chef’s knives laid out in a neat row. An icebox—thick wood with black iron strapping—stood on the other side of the wooden table. Along the other three walls there was gray Formica countertop over cabinetry painted white. Above that, open pantry shelves held bulk foods packaged in plastic bags, canned foods, fruit jars, store bread, and several bags of chips and snack food.

On the counters, Spiegle had a can opener on a metal stand, a breadbox of pinewood, a hand juicer for oranges, tins of coffee and flour, and a small lazy Susan, holding two tiers of store-bought spices. Beside the sink, Spiegle had clamped a hand-cranked meat grinder to the countertop. In the center of the room stood a kitchen table and four plain chairs in golden-maple finish, and on the kitchen table sat a portable radio, showing AM and FM bands, with a separate dial for shortwave frequencies.

Wilsher turned back to face the bishop and asked, “Did you know he used a radio?”

Shetler frowned. “He wasn’t supposed to. We were working on that.”

“You mean that he should have gotten rid of it?”

“Yes,” Shetler said and studied the black box. “But this one is bigger than the one I knew about.”

“He’s got a smaller one,” Wilsher said. “In the bedroom, upstairs.”

Shetler pulled at his chin whiskers. “Did he have a phone, too?”

“In his pants pocket,” Wilsher said. “We’re going through his call history, but it’s a prepaid phone from Walmart with no owner's registration. The memory chip will have his address book."

Distracted by his thoughts, Shetler looked back at Wilsher and said, "What?"

"We're checking his call history. To see who he was talking to."

"You can do that?" Shetler asked.

"Yes."

"But really, is that something the government is allowed to do?"

"If we have the proper warrants."

Shetler shook his head. "Everybody has those phones, now. I don't think they know the government can check their calls."

"It's all in the phone company computers," Wilsher said. He stepped out through the back door and down a short flight of steps to the backyard—a small patch of lawn with a concrete walkway leading to a shed for Spiegle's horses and a barn off to one side. In the shade of the horse shed, Wilsher pointed out a Honda gasoline generator mounted on a wooden platform, and he asked Shetler, "Would he be permitted to run anything electrical with this?"

Shetler answered, "He kept a few batteries charged up, for lights here and there. But he wasn't supposed to use them much. It was just going to be a temporary thing, until he adjusted to plain life."

In the barn, Wilsher showed Spiegle's buggy to Shetler and said, "He's got one of those batteries mounted under his buggy, Bishop."

Shetler bent over to look. Attached to the undercarriage, in front of the rear oval springs, Spiegle had a shelf holding a 12-volt car battery.

Standing up straight, Shetler smiled in mild consternation and said, "He was still making some adjustments to plain living, Chief Deputy. We were working on things like this."

Outside in the barnyard, Wilsher asked, "Was he well treated? Did people out here accept him?"

"We were working on that, too."

"Did he have any particular friends?"

"He had the whole church, I suppose."

"But did he spend time with anyone in particular?"

"Me, I guess. And Billy Winters. But mostly he kept to himself."

"How'd he get his house built?"

"He hired some of it done. We helped him with the rest."

"And the outbuildings? Same thing?"

"He bought the lumber, and we put it up for him."

"So, people had accepted him?"

"So to speak."

"Did he farm?"

"No. He leased his land to other men, so they could raise a cash crop."

"Did he make a lot of money doing that?"

"Not really. That wasn't the point."

"Why didn't he farm the land himself?"

Shetler took off his black felt hat and wiped his white brow with a bandanna from the side pocket of his pants. Holding his hat at his thigh, he looked up at the blue sky and then across the wide pastoral valley to the eastern horizon. Brown fields of tall corn and soybean stubble stretched as far as the eye could see. On the horizon, a tall red barn stood out against the blue sky. The wavy line of a creek bed wandered through the valley, and on all of the hills, between the fields, there blazed the red, yellow, and orange of autumn leaves. Looking back to Wilsher, Shetler replaced his hat and said, "Glenn wasn't really interested in farming."

"Then what did he do with himself?"

"He kept to himself, mostly. Sunday meetings were a little bit like that, too. I mean, he kept to himself."

"So, other than Billy Winters, he didn't have any close friends?"

"I guess not. Jacob Miller spent some time over here, but that's about all."

"Did he have any enemies?"

Shetler seemed surprised by the question. "Certainly not."

"Well, Bishop, after all, he was murdered."

"Crist Burkholder was not his enemy."

"No, I guess not. Except that he beat the man to death."

Shetler shook his head and did not reply.

Wilsher pointed out the empty horse shed and asked, "Where are the buggy horses?"

"I arranged for one of the Detweiler boys to take them."

Shading his eyes, Wilsher asked, "Did you *arrange* to have anything else taken away?"

Shetler blushed. "The horses need to be looked after, Chief Deputy."

"But nothing else was taken?"

"No."

"Who will get the farm, Bishop?"

"I haven't decided. One of the young couples. Someone who needs a farm, if they're going to get married."

"Where are his bank accounts?"

"I don't think he has any."

"That's strange, don't you think?"

"Not really."

"OK," Wilsher said, "he has no natural heirs, and he's left everything in his will to you."

"Did you find his will?"

Wilsher nodded. "All of his papers were in a box in his bedroom closet—up on a high shelf. And we've read through everything. So far as we can tell, he hasn't got a bank account."

Shetler nodded. "He shouldn't have needed one."

"Maybe. But he also hasn't got any credit cards. No bills at a store. No charge accounts."

"He wouldn't need those," Shetler said evenly, putting his hat back on his head. He stuffed his bandanna back into his side pants pocket and added, "Glenn Spiegle always paid cash."

"Don't you think that's a bit strange, Bishop?"

"Why? What's strange about an Amishman using cash?"

Wilsher studied the short man, smiled, and said, "Because, Bishop, if he always paid cash, where did he keep his money?"

"I don't follow you."

"Bishop, we haven't found any money."

"Well, I know he always had plenty of cash."

"OK, but where is it? We've searched the house, the barn, everywhere. Unless he's got it buried in cans out in a field somewhere, we can't find any evidence that he actually had any money."

Shetler shrugged an honest uncertainty, lifted his palms, and said, "I don't know."

"Can you tell me why Spiegle came up here, Bishop?"

"He wanted peace," Shetler said. "He said he wanted to hide away in a peaceful place, and forget about his past."

"How'd he choose Holmes County?"

"Billy Winters brought him up," the bishop said, starting around the back corner of the house.

Wilsher followed and said, "We know what he did, Bishop. We've checked."

The bishop stopped in the shade beside the house and looked up at Wilsher. "The cruelest torture in life, Chief Deputy, is remorse."

Wilsher nodded. "He killed a young girl, Bishop. DUI Vehicular Homicide, and he spent eighteen years in prison for it."

"That's why he was here. He wanted forgiveness. He wanted to learn how to forgive himself."

"He could have done that in Florida, Bishop."

Shetler tipped his chin, agreeing. "Billy Winters once said that Spiegle needed to escape his memories. That he needed to be able to make a clean start someplace where his memories couldn't torture him. So, that's extreme remorse operating there, Chief Deputy. That's the kind of remorse that keeps you from being able to forgive yourself."

"Was he making any progress on that, Mr. Shetler?"

"We were working on that, too."

"You were *working on* a lot of things."

Shetler did not respond.

"I'm curious, Mr. Shetler. What did you tell him about forgiving himself? And if he killed a girl in Florida, why would he insist so strongly that he had to marry Vesta Miller? If he were remorseful about one girl, why would he press his interests so strongly with another girl, who plainly didn't want him?"

"I don't know, Chief Deputy. I don't understand that, any more than the next man."

Wilsher nodded, thought. "And the remorse? How were you helping him with that?"

"I told him what I could," Shetler said, and stalled, looking out over the valley.

"Which is?" Wilsher prompted.

"Outside of grace," Shetler said, turning back to Wilsher, "this type of forgiveness isn't possible."

"Which means what?"

"It means that we need God's help, if we are to find this level of forgiveness. We need His help, because outside of grace, we don't deserve to be forgiven."

16

Wednesday, October 7
4:45 P.M.

AT HIS small church in Millersburg, Cal finished making preparations for Wednesday evening services by setting out one-page worship programs in the vestibule. Then he crossed the gravel parking lot to the white-frame parsonage, and entered by the kitchen door. His daughter Rachel, a dwarf woman in her early forties, was standing on an elevated platform at the stove, stirring a pan of soup.

Cal had designed the platform so that Rachel could wheel it around the kitchen and then step onto it to settle it down onto its spring-loaded pads. The rolling box had a single step, and both the step and the top of the box were painted with a black, rubberized, nonslip coating. Rachel had painted the rest of the box her favorite color—the yellow of a summer goldfinch. She had the radio turned to an oldies station in Wooster, which was playing a Rolling Stones retrospective, and Cal came into the kitchen to the loud, slow pulse of Mick Jagger's "Satisfaction."

Stepping down from her box, Rachel turned the radio off and said, "Everybody's talking about Glenn Spiegle, Dad. You been out there?"

"Earlier," Cal said. "Then I was down at the jail, some."

As Cal started to set the table for dinner, Rachel asked, "Does Burkholder have a lawyer?"

"Linda Hart," Cal said. "She thinks he's innocent."

"Didn't he confess?" Rachel asked.

Round and short, Rachel showed more age than her years. Her hair was graying, her face showed long, deep creases beside her chin, and her complexion was pale and pocked in several places from childhood chickenpox scars.

Taking water glasses down from a high shelf, Cal said, "Yes, he confessed. But Hart doesn't believe it."

"Why not, Dad? It seems straightforward."

"Crist says he remembers hitting Spiegle only once."

Rachel shook her head. "Robertson's gonna argue that he lost it, Dad. He's gonna say Burkholder beat him to death, and he just can't remember it."

"That's about the size of it," Cal said. He pulled napkins out of a drawer and added, "But Hart's not conceding."

"She's not stupid," Rachel said and mounted her box again. She brought the soup pan down from the stove, and set it on a trivet at the kitchen table. "Are his hands wrecked?" she asked and climbed up to sit on her chair.

Cal served soup into two bowls and sat across from Rachel. "I don't have all the details."

"If his hands aren't wrecked, Dad, then someone else killed Spiegle."

"Could be," Cal said and tasted the soup.

"How's Darba Winters taking all this?" Rachel asked. "She holding it together?"

"Not so well, really," Cal said. "She needs Billy to come home. Then she'll be OK."

Rachel ate her soup and said, "He takes his time coming home."

"How do you know that?"

"His truck is still parked at Bradenton Beach. I've got its GPS location on my computer, and it hasn't moved since two o'clock."

Cal smiled and shook his head, and Rachel said, "You think I'd let that much cheese leave the factory without a transponder? All our trucks are tagged, Dad. I can tell you where each of them is, at any time."

Cal laughed. "The Klines didn't know what they were getting into, when they hired you."

"They said they wanted to 'get modern,' Dad."

"Yeah?" Cal said, setting his soup bowl aside. "So, show me."

Rachel hopped off her chair and led Cal into her tech room. At the monitor, she double-clicked on Google Earth, typed in GPS coordinates, and brought up a stretch of Bradenton Beach, where a small parking lot for a water's-edge restaurant fronted a stretch of white sand along Gulf Coast Drive.

Standing behind Rachel, Cal studied the scene, shadows long on the ground, and asked, "So, where's your truck?"

Rachel put her cursor over the top of a thick stand of trees at the north end of the parking lot and said, "This is the location of my transponder." Then with her finger, she pointed out the edge of the trees, and she said, "There's where my truck is, Dad. Parked under the trees."

Cal looked and said, "I don't see anything there."

"This isn't a real-time display, Dad. It's a satellite image that could have been made months ago. I just know where my transponder is located, and that's where its GPS coordinates are. Right there, under those trees."

Little interested in the technology, Cal sat in a reading chair in the corner and said, "Darba says he goes out to that beach every time he drives down there. He sits and waits for the sunset."

"I know," Rachel said, as she moved the cursor to pan up and down the beach. "Then he drives back up US 77, and stops to sleep for a couple of hours in Virginia."

Standing up, Cal said, "Can you let me know when he moves his truck? Maybe give me a call?" He turned for the door.

"He never moves until after dark, Dad."

"OK, but will you know when he does move?"

"Yes. His GPS transponder will show it."

"OK, that'd be something I could tell Darba," Cal said. "It might help her calm down a bit."

"Ok, Dad, where you gonna be after church?"

"Over at the Brandens'."

"Isn't the professor on sabbatical?"

"Yes," Cal said. "Down at Duke."

"So?"

"Caroline's home this week."

"What do you want with her?"

"I thought she'd like to go out to see an Amish couple with me tomorrow," Cal said, turning back to the room. "Over in the Doughty Valley."

Rachel turned back to face her computer screen, and Cal asked, "Can you help a friend of mine learn the Internet?"

Rachel turned back to him. "Who?"

"You'd have to keep it a secret."

"Why?"

"He's that kind of fellow, is all."

"What kind of help does he need?"

"FTP servers. Navigating sites."

"You're kidding."

"A little, yes, but he needs to know more about Internet protocols. He can't get by with just the basics anymore."

"You going to tell me who it is, Dad?"

"If you can do this without letting anyone know about it."

"OK, who?"

"Bruce Robertson," Cal smiled.

Rachel came off her chair. "You're kidding!"

"You've got to keep it a secret, Rachel."

"I'll blackmail the creep," Rachel blurted.

"You can't do that, Rachel."

"You want me to help the *giant* sheriff of this *whole* big county learn to click a *mouse* through the Internet, and I can't *talk* about it?"

"Right."

"Can't do that, Dad."

"A favor to me?"

"Dad!"

"No, I'm serious. Maybe he could come over here for lessons. You'd have him fixed up in no time."

"Sheriff Robertson sitting here, next to a dwarf woman computer geek, and I can't even take a picture?"

"It has to be secret."

Rachel thought, ruffled her hair with her short fingers, and whistled. "Dad," she said. "Are you serious?"

"If he gives you any trouble," Cal smiled, "you just show him who's boss. A couple of stern scoldings, and I guarantee you Bruce Robertson will come apart like a cheap toy."

"Oh, you *guarantee* it, do you?"

"Well, not me. That's what Linda Hart says about Robertson—that he'll come apart like a cheap toy."

Smiling mischief, Rachel said, "I'll do it, if you let me tell Linda about it."

Cal hesitated.

"I tell Linda," Rachel said, "or no deal."

"All right, but you have to wait until the Burkholder case is finished."

"I don't think I can do that, Dad."

"That, or no deal, Rachel."

"OK. After the Burkholder case is finished, I get to tell Linda Hart, right?"

"After the Burkholder case," Cal said, "you can post it on the Internet for all I care."

17

Thursday, October 8
9:20 A.M.

WITH CAROLINE Branden beside him the next morning, Cal drove his gray work truck up the hill and around the long horseshoe bend on Route 83 south of Millersburg. They came out of the ascending curve and dropped down off the high forest passage, traveled through several miles of open farmland, crossed lazy Bucks Run under a canopy of tall oaks and white-trunked sycamores, and turned east onto County 19, skirting the Doughty Creek. The road meandered through several miles of woodland and then came out into the wide Doughty Valley, where long stretches of field corn stood browning in the morning sun. One farm after another passed by, as Cal drove east along the curving lane—slowing at the crest of each hill, watching for the road apples that would mark the recent passage of a horse and buggy.

Considerably taller than the pastor, Caroline sat beside Cal and brushed absently with her fingertips at the curls of her long auburn hair, wondering how they would find Sara and Jeremiah Miller to be, raising their young family on Bishop Eli Miller's old farm. She wondered, also, how they'd find Vesta Miller to be that morning. Cal had taken Vesta out to the Millers' farm the night before, after Wednesday evening services, and then he had stopped at the Brandens' house to tell Caroline about the murder of Glenn Spiegle.

Breaking into her thoughts, Cal said, "Vesta will probably want a ride into town this morning."

"What?" Caroline asked, as Cal swung into the Millers' drive.

"I think we'll need to give Vesta a ride into town," Cal said. "To see Crist."

Caroline nodded and pointed ahead, as Cal pulled to a stop on the drive. At the end of the short drive, Jeremiah stood with his uncle Isaac in front of an RV the size of a Greyhound bus.

The two Amish men looked like a matched set of twins, their black chin whiskers round and full against their chests. Black felt hats covered identical Dutch-boy haircuts. Blue denim trousers matched their plain denim vests, hanging open in front over dark blue shirts. And side by side, the two men stood in front of the big RV wearing smiles that broke from ear to ear across their round, farm-tanned faces.

Cal parked on the drive and got out to shake hands with the men. Caroline followed behind him, and the two Amish men nodded bashful greetings to her. Knowing Amish reservations well, Caroline suppressed an urge to give Jeremiah a hug. Instead, she asked simply, "Is Sara here?" and angled toward the front porch. As she spoke, Sara came out on the porch and waved. Caroline climbed the front steps and slipped through the front door, turning back briefly to wave to Cal.

Once the two women were inside, Cal asked about the RV, and Jeremiah smiled, saying, "Sara's former bishop got a lot of money from the Spits Wallace estate."

"So, he bought an RV?" Cal asked.

"Bought some land, first," Isaac responded. "Then the RV, so we could share it around."

"Made any trips in it yet?" Cal asked.

Jeremiah led them over to the front porch and said, "This will be our first trip, Cal. Disney World. All of Isaac's family, and all of mine."

"You know how to drive it?" Cal asked.

"I've practiced some."

"Got a driver's license?" Cal asked.

Jeremiah smiled an evasive answer, but didn't speak.

Cal shook his head and stepped up onto the front porch behind Isaac and Jeremiah. The men took seats in hickory rockers, and as soon as they sat down, Sara toed the screened door open and asked, "Coffee?"

Jeremiah and Isaac shook their heads, but Cal said, "Sure, thanks," and Sara went back inside.

Leaning forward, Cal said, "How is Vesta Miller?"

"She took a buggy into town already," Isaac said, shaking his head. "To see Crist."

Sara pushed the screened door open, came out onto the porch, and handed Cal a mug of black coffee. When she turned to go back inside, Cal noticed that her left toes dragged a little behind her leg, and after she went back inside, he asked, "Sara still having trouble from her strokes?"

Jeremiah nodded. "She still has trouble with the letters V and W. Her cheek droops a little. And she drags her leg when she's tired."

Cal tasted his coffee and asked, "How are the kids?"

"Fine," Jeremiah said evenly. "Excited about the trip."

Cal laughed. "I'd like to have a picture of that. You know—a picture of all you Amish, down at Disney."

Blank stares came from the two Amish men.

Covering the silence, Cal assured them, "I wouldn't try to take your pictures."

Jeremiah nodded and laughed. Eyes dancing, Isaac said, "We're just givin' you the business, Cal."

A peaceful, silent moment passed as the men rocked on the front porch, and then Jeremiah said, "Vesta's father could smell money through an iron door."

Slow to catch his thoughts up to that remark, Cal asked, "You know about him?"

Jeremiah nodded. "He's been trying to get one of his daughters married into our district."

Cal sipped his coffee and let another moment pass silently, knowing to let the men speak of Crist and Vesta when they were ready. They spoke of the weather, the crops, and the RV trip to Disney, and then, casting his gaze out over a distant field of corn, Jeremiah remarked, "Crist Burkholder was gonna be a big problem for Jacob Miller."

Cal waited a beat, sipped some more coffee, and then carefully asked, "Because he wanted Vesta to marry Glenn Spiegle, instead of Crist Burkholder?"

Both Isaac and Jeremiah nodded.

"OK," Cal asked, "but what did Glenn Spiegle have that Vesta's father would have been so interested in?"

After a silence, Jeremiah answered, "Money, Cal. A lot of money, even by your English standards."

* * *

"She's still impaired, Cal," Caroline complained sadly.

They were in Cal's battered truck, driving back to Millersburg in a thunderstorm that was producing sleet, the pulse of the ice on the old metal roof sounding like a thousand wooden mallets pounding loose stone.

"She drags her left foot, Cal," Caroline added over the rattle of the storm. "And her cheek is still sunken."

"I know," Cal said. "I should have prepared you better."

Agitated, Caroline turned on her seat to face Cal and said, "A doctor told her that it's dangerous for her to have children, but the bishop won't let her use birth control."

"How do you know that?"

"She told me, Cal. She wants me to help her get birth control. She says Vesta wants it, too, but they can't tell anyone. The church doesn't *permit* it."

"Amish don't use birth control, Caroline. You know that."

"But this is Sara, Cal. She's had strokes, and she shouldn't have any more kids."

Cal slowed at the junction with Route 83 and waited in the mounting storm for a buggy to clear the intersection. The sleet turned to rain, and Cal made the turn, with dark clouds pressing close to the road and the rain coming down so hard that it produced a spray on the pavement in front of his truck. Choosing his words carefully, Cal drove slowly through the rain and said, "Did you know that Isaac leaves money for artificial insemination in a secret place, behind a post in his barn?"

"What?" Caroline asked over the pounding of the rain.

"I'm trying to tell you something about birth control," Cal said as he steered through standing water. "With the Amish, Caroline. Isaac has to pay secretly for artificial insemination."

"What in the world are you talking about?"

They passed through a brief clearing and then through another burst of cold rain.

"For the cows, Caroline. They're not allowed to use artificial insemination for the cows."

"What has that got to do with Vesta?"

"It goes against nature," Cal said, "so it's not allowed. But they need it to sustain their herds. So at a prearranged time, all of Isaac's family manages to be away from home, and they put the "candidate" in one of the milking stalls in the barn. Then the man comes to do his work. If he's sure nobody's home, he goes into the barn, does his thing, and takes his fee from the hiding place behind the post. It gives Isaac plausible deniability, and the bishop never has to know about it. Or at least he never has a reason to ask about it. And if he doesn't ask, they can all pretend that he doesn't know about it."

"Seems hypocritical to me," Caroline snapped.

Noting her tone, Cal said, "If they're going to have birth control—Sara and Vesta—someone's going to have to help them do it secretly."

Fighting her emotions, Caroline rode beside Cal and tried to suppress her anxiety by listening to the rumbling of the thunder overhead and to the splashing of Cal's truck tires as he drove through the standing water on the pavement.

Cal's phone rang, and as he steered, he checked the display and answered it, saying, "Hi, Rachel."

He listened, said, "OK," switched off, and said to Caroline, "Can you come over to the house? I need to stop at home."

Caroline shook her head. "Just take me home, Cal."

"You're upset about Sara?"

"I don't know. I guess. Things seem to make me angry, anymore."

"You going to be OK?"

"Yes," Caroline answered halfheartedly. "Really, Cal, you should just take me home."

Cal drove into town past the Walmart and said, "Is this more of your recent anxiety?"

"I don't know. It's probably just Sara and Vesta. You know, not being able to use birth control."

"Because, if it's more of that anxiety," Cal continued, "then maybe we should talk."

Caroline didn't answer right away. They made the turn at the courthouse square, and Caroline said, "It's just ignorance, Cal. With the Amish. It makes me angry. Lots of things seem to make me angry, anymore."

"This isn't like you," Cal said. "Have you talked with Mike? About feeling this anger, again?"

"This isn't about Eddie, Cal," Caroline said. "It's just Sara and Vesta. And Vesta's father. And Crist Burkholder in jail, because her father wouldn't let her marry him. All of it, I guess. And now, Sara needs help with something that ought to be easy."

"Are you sure that's all it is? You had that angry spell, after you killed Eddie."

"Please, just take me home, Cal."

"You should come over to my house," Cal offered again.

"Doesn't Rachel need you? Didn't she just call?"

"Yes, but I think you could use the company."

"Please, Cal. This isn't about Eddie Hunt-Myers."

Cal made the turn onto the college heights and pulled into the Brandens' cul-de-sac. When Caroline got out, she wouldn't turn to him to say good-bye. But, in the corner of her eye, Cal saw the tears starting to form.

18

Thursday, October 8
11:30 A.M.

RACHEL RAMSAYER was not a particularly small dwarf, but she was still nowhere near average in height. When she was seated at her computer, her feet touched the floor only because Cal had made adjustments to the legs and casters on her chair. And he had built the custom office furniture in her study, with a computer console set lower to the floor than average. So when he pulled his taller chair up to her monitor, she had to adjust its angle so they both could see it.

"Here it is," she said, and clicked open her Google Earth program. Then with several clicks of her mouse, she drew down her focus successively closer to the stretch of beach in Bradenton where Billy Winters's truck transponder had been located the day before.

Once Cal had a chance to study the scene, Rachel said, "I had the Bradenton Beach police on the phone, Dad. All the excitement's over, but that's where Billy's truck is. I mean, it's still there, and it shouldn't be."

"Your tracker—transponder—says it's still there?"

"Yes. The police station is two blocks away. I've been talking with a local cop, and he says they've got the truck roped off with crime scene tape, and they're going through it right now."

Cal asked, "Do we know where Billy is?"

"No, and the police don't know, either."

"And they're wondering why his truck is still there?" Cal asked, tapping the screen.

"More than that, Dad. They've been on this scene since about eleven o'clock last night."

"Why?"

"Someone reported an *incident.*"

"What is that, exactly?"

"An 'incident' is all they said."

"But the truck is still there, Rachel."

"Right, Dad. They've had the crime scene people out there all night."

"Why? Is Billy hurt?"

"Don't know, Dad, but there's blood on the inside panel of the driver's-side door. And the door was left hanging open, like there was a fight, and Billy ran off."

Cal pushed back and stood up to pace the room. "What else do you know?"

Rachel turned her chair toward Cal. "Police are interviewing the witness who reported the incident. They had to track him down with phone records, because he wouldn't give his name when he called 911."

"So, somebody saw something. That's good."

"Yes, but I don't know who that is, yet. And I don't know what he's telling the police down there."

Stopping in the center of the room, Cal asked, "Does Darba Winters know anything about this?"

"I don't know, but I called Evelyn Carson this morning, as soon as I got off the phone with Bradenton Beach."

"Did she go out to Darba's place?"

"I think so."

"OK, do you have any other way to find out about Billy?"

"No. I'd have to hack the police computers."

"You can do that?"

"Of course I could. Question is, would you really want me to do that?"

"Probably not."

"Good call, Dad."

"Do you still have a phone contact?"

"Sure, but anybody can call down there, Dad. There's only a few cops in the unit at Bradenton Beach."

"OK, what do we know so far? Let's go through it."

"The truck's been there all night. Right where Billy parked it, yesterday."

"But, we don't really know that Billy is the one who parked it there," Cal argued.

"OK, it's right where Billy *usually* parks it."

"What else?"

"Police are there, investigating."

"What else?"

"Somebody was hurt. There's blood. Not much, but there definitely is blood."

Cal headed out of the room slowly. Thinking. Frowning.

"Where you going, Dad?"

Absently, Cal answered, "Out to see Evelyn Carson."

"At Darba Winters's place?"

Cal turned back. "Right."

"You want me to stay on this?"

"You don't have to go to work?"

"I can work from home today."

"OK, then can you let me know what the police find?"

"Sure."

"And what happens to that truck?"

"That'd be my responsibility, anyway. To keep track of the truck."

"But the police, too, right? You'll check with the police, about Billy?"

"Yes, but that's my truck down there. So, I called Bruce Robertson, and he called Bradenton Beach to tell them I'd be following the case for Kline's Cheese. And he asked for cooperation, keeping him informed, too."

"Wait," Cal said and thought. "Does Robertson know that Billy's missing?"

"We don't really know that Billy *is actually missing,* Dad."

"Right, but there's blood in his truck."

"Doesn't mean that Billy is missing. Not yet, anyway. That could be anybody's blood."

"But, blood is not good."

"No."

"OK, then I'm still going out to Darba's place."

"You should go see Bruce, first."

"Why?"

"He wants to talk to you about Crist Burkholder."

"Is there a problem?"

"Aside from the fact that he killed someone?"

Cal grimaced. "*Apart from the fact that a pacifist Amish lad killed someone with his fists,* do you know what Robertson wants?"

"No, but he said Missy Taggert has finished her autopsy. And he wants to ask you a few questions."

"OK. Robertson first, then Darba."

"Right, Dad. But the sheriff was gonna have his first computer lesson here at six o'clock. And now, I'm thinking that I probably should wave him off."

19

Thursday, October 8
1:00 P.M.

CAL ATE lunch at the McDonald's south of town and drove up to the courthouse square, turning into narrow Court Street behind the jail. A clergy pass would normally let him park anywhere he wanted at the jail, but Cal had never bothered to request one. As it was, every deputy in Holmes County knew his battered gray carpenter's truck, and when he pulled to the curb, he knew with reasonable certainty that he'd never get a ticket, despite the several "Sheriff's Vehicles Only" signs that were bolted to the brick walls. Aside from the sheriff and his deputies, Professor Michael Branden was the only other person in Holmes County who was afforded that same rare privilege to park behind the jail.

Inside, Cal walked down the old paneled hallway past the deputy's ready room to Robertson's office on the left, and before he pushed through the door, he gave a wave to Ellie Troyer-Niell, who was working one of the radio consoles at her desk at the end of the hall. She waved him a go-ahead, and Cal knocked and entered.

Robertson was standing at one of the west-facing windows of his office, back turned to the room, watching traffic roll by on Clay Street, just south of its busy intersection with Jackson. Once in the room, Cal could see the Civil War monument through the windows to the north, and against the wall to the right of Robertson's door, he found Missy Taggert, standing beside the credenza, pouring herself a cup of coffee.

Missy's curly brown hair was pinned up in back, and she was dressed in her medical examiner's green scrubs and a pair of soft white shoes. Cal nodded, Missy said, "Hi, Cal," and they both took seats at the front edge of Robertson's big cherry desk. When the sheriff turned from the window, he asked Cal, "You get my message?"

"Rachel said you have some questions."

Robertson nodded and stepped behind his desk to drop his bulk into his swivel chair.

While the sheriff pulled himself up to his desk, Missy said, "I've finished my autopsy, Cal."

Cal nodded and looked to Robertson. The sheriff hesitated and then brought forward his chief complaint.

"Cal," he said, "this confession doesn't square with the autopsy."

Missy said, "Spiegle was beaten so severely, Cal, that five bones in his face were crushed."

Robertson asked, "You ever know an Amish kid to *go off* on someone like that?"

"It's hard for me to believe that any of them would do that," Cal said.

"They're farmhands, Cal. They'd be strong enough."

"Strength is one thing," Cal said. "But they're pacifists. At least they're supposed to be."

"Then we've got one who isn't," Robertson said, and pushed back from his desk. "Tell him, Missy."

Matter-of-factly, Missy said, "Spiegle's face was battered and almost unrecognizable. But first, he fell and hit his head on the concrete pad inside that barn. It was the subsequent beating that killed him. He blew out an aneurysm, which he probably already had—they can be genetic in origin, so he may have had it all his life—and that resulted in a subdural hematoma. He would have died in minutes."

"Crist told me that he hit him only once," Cal said.

Robertson scoffed, "Then either he's lying, or he doesn't remember. Either way, it's manslaughter."

Missy nodded agreement over her coffee cup. "If Burkholder beat him up after he fell—like my autopsy shows—then he killed him. It's really quite simple, Cal."

"But isn't it likely that any beating at all would have killed him?" Cal asked.

"Can't say," Missy said. "But this wasn't just any beating, Cal. This was merciless."

Cal thought about Crist Burkholder holding that much rage in a fistfight and wondered why Glenn Spiegle wouldn't have defended himself. Maybe the first blow had incapacitated him. He wondered also why Crist Burkholder was so intent on confessing.

Robertson said, "The problem we have now is that Burkholder's hands are not bruised. They aren't even scratched. It doesn't look like he beat up anyone."

Cal looked to Missy and then back to the sheriff. "Are you saying that you think he's innocent?"

"I do," Missy said. "I think he hit him once, and ran off, like he says."

Cal looked to Robertson. The sheriff nodded and said, "I don't really want to charge him."

Cal lifted his palms. "So, what's the problem?"

"His confession," Robertson said. "He's not retracting his confession."

"What does Linda Hart say?" Cal asked.

"She won't let us talk to him anymore," Robertson said.

"Does she know that you don't believe his confession?" Cal asked.

Robertson held up a hand. "It's only Missy who doesn't believe it, Cal. I think he beat the man, and he just doesn't remember it."

"But his hands aren't damaged," Cal argued.

"So," Robertson said, "he was wearing gloves."

"So, where are they?" Cal asked.

Robertson rolled his eyes and stood up. "Come on, Cal. He disposed of them."

"OK," Cal said. "But if he's clever enough to hide a bloody pair of gloves, why does he insist on confessing?"

"I don't know," Robertson sighed out. "It probably doesn't matter, anyway."

"Why?" Cal asked.

"Linda Hart has asked for a Miranda hearing this afternoon. She's filed a motion to toss out Burkholder's confession altogether."

* * *

As he left the sheriff's office, Cal turned in the doorway and asked Robertson, "Are you following the Billy Winters disappearance?"

Robertson laughed. "Cal, he probably just wandered off somewhere, drunk. He probably just finally fell off the wagon."

"I don't know," Cal said. "They found blood inside his truck."

Robertson shrugged his lack of interest. "All I did was call down to let them know whose truck it is. I haven't really been paying attention."

Missy stood up and said, "I've got to drive back up to the hospital," and moved toward the door, apparently not much interested in Billy Winters, either.

Robertson saw her out to the front entrance and came back to his office to find Cal standing in front of the desk, pensive.

Cal turned for the door again and said, "Rachel is going to follow the Bradenton Beach police investigation. I think you should do that, too."

Robertson acknowledged that with a tip of his head and stepped back behind his desk.

On his way through the door, Cal muttered, "I'm going out to check on Darba Winters. She's worried about Billy."

Robertson said to his back, "I'll call Bradenton Beach, Cal, but Billy Winters is a drunk. Always will be."

Cal turned back to say, "I've got to believe in someone today, Bruce."

Scoffing, Robertson said, "Amish murderers, Cal. Who'd believe in that?"

20

Thursday, October 8
2:20 P.M.

WHEN CAL pulled up at Darba Winters's place, Bishop Leon Shetler was sitting in his plain black buggy, parked on the lane in front. Cal swung his gray truck into Darba's drive and walked back to stand beside the bishop's rig. On the high seat of the buggy, the bishop looked down at Cal and said, "My Katie is inside," shaking his head.

"Visiting?" Cal asked.

"You don't know?" Shetler asked, surprised.

"Know what?"

"Darba tore her place apart about an hour ago," the bishop said, pointing out scratches on his arms and a bruise under his eye. "I had to help the doctor settle her down."

"What do you mean, she 'tore her place apart'?" Cal said, as he turned to walk across the lawn toward the house.

Shetler climbed out of his buggy and followed, saying, "Katie and I were already here when the doctor arrived. We were visiting, and Darba was still pretty worried about Billy."

Cal stopped. "Evie was supposed to tell her that they found Billy's truck."

"Dr. Carson told Darba that his truck hadn't been moved since last night, and the police found blood. Then Darba got nuts. Throwing chairs, tipping over tables, breaking plates, smashing china, punching holes in the walls. Swinging fists, too," Shetler added, rubbing the bruise on his cheek.

The men climbed the two short steps up onto the front stoop. When Cal started to pull the screened door open, Evelyn Carson met them at the door and said, "I can't let you in."

"You need help?" Cal asked.

"Don't think so," Carson said, "but Darba should be sleeping. I gave her a sedative, but she's still up on her feet, crying about Billy. She says we've got to call him, and tell him not to ever come back here."

From the back hallway, they heard Darba screaming, "You run, Billy! You run, boy!"

"What does that mean?" Cal asked.

"She acts like someone's after him," Carson said. "She's been screaming like that since I told her that Billy is missing."

21

Thursday, October 8
2:30 P.M.

ON THE second floor of the old jail, in the narrow bricked hallway several paces down from Crist Burkholder's cell door, Linda Hart stood whispering with Vesta Miller. Dressed in her usual black suit, the angular lawyer was a head taller than Vesta, and she leaned in to speak earnestly.

"Just try to get him to trust me, Vesta," Hart said. "He needs to let me handle the judge."

"OK," Vesta said, "but Crist can be stubborn. And I'm not sure what you want me to say to him."

Vesta wore a full-length cotton dress of a soft lilac color. Her white bonnet covered the bun at the back of her head, and her white day apron hung in front, nearly as long as her dress, which covered her legs to the tops of her ankles. She twisted a lace hankie in her fingers, needing the normal—housework, cooking, anything but this. Anything but these brick walls. Anything but an English jail.

But here she was, she told herself, and there was nothing to be done about it now. So listen, Vesta, she thought. Listen to the imposing lawyer, dressed all in black. Let this English lawyer juggle this thoroughly English dilemma.

The trouble was, it would be English people now who would juggle the fate of all the rest of her years. It was the English people and their courts who would lock Crist away for all the rest of his life. For all the rest of her life. But the lawyer woman was so certain of herself. So confident that Crist would not go to jail.

Was that possible? Could that really happen? Or was her new life with Crist Burkholder already done and finished, before they had even gotten started?

"Just tell him to trust me," Linda Hart was saying. "Tell him that I can get his confession tossed out."

"He won't go to prison?" Vesta asked.

"Vesta, I don't think he'll even go to trial. Much less be convicted."

"But, what if he really did do it?"

"I don't know anything about that," Hart said, leaning closer. "We haven't come to that yet. First, I want to get his confession tossed out. Then, maybe he won't even go to trial."

"He says he did it," Vesta argued, hoping the lawyer could convince her to find hope where Vesta suspected none could exist.

"Vesta," Hart said, and pulled the girl down the hall toward Crist Burkholder's cell door. "Even the coroner doesn't believe he did it. But that's not the question we need to address right now. First, we need to win this Miranda hearing. Then we'll see what happens."

"Because the sheriff didn't tell him his rights?"

"Yes."

"Why would that matter, if Crist says he did it?"

"Because, without his Miranda warning, Crist never really did *confess* that he did it. At least not as far as the law is concerned."

"But he *did* confess."

"Not if we win this argument."

Vesta stopped in the hall and considered that. "What do you want me to say to him?"

At the end of the hallway, Ricky Niell appeared, and Hart leaned down to Vesta and put her finger to her lips.

Niell walked up to them, and Hart said, "Ricky, I want Vesta to talk to him, before I do."

"I'd have to sit in on that," Ricky said.

"You can watch through the mirror, Sergeant, but I can't let you listen."

Ricky nodded. "I'll take him to Interview B."

* * *

On the first floor of the jail, while Hart waited in the hallway outside Interview B, Vesta sat at the long gray table in front of the one-way mirror, and told Crist what his lawyer had said to her.

Crist sat across from her in his orange jailhouse jumpsuit, and considered the implications of what she had told him. He balanced the truth of what he knew against the legalisms of the English law, and he wondered if it were that way in all the rest of America. Could it be true? Kill a man and go scot-free because of something the sheriff hadn't said at the time of his arrest?

He reached across the table for Vesta's hands, and said, "I have to live with the truth of what I did, Vesta."

"I know, Crist," Vesta said. "But maybe you don't have to go to prison."

"She doesn't care if I did it?"

"She says the Miranda hearing has to be first. Then maybe they won't believe your confession."

"But I know it's true, Vesta."

"I know," Vesta said and pulled her hands back across the table. "But think about our lives, Crist."

"You could live with this?"

"I want to live with you."

"That was all a dream, Vesta. It was a dream we had once, before I killed a man."

Vesta studied Crist's eyes for encouragement. She studied them for reassurance. For hope. But he looked back at her without any of those blessings showing in his gaze.

"What are you going to do, Crist?"

Burkholder reached again for her hands, took them into his, and said, "I don't know."

22

Thursday, October 8
3:00 P.M.

IN THE courtroom of Judge Robert Knowles, Crist sat with his lawyer at the defense table in front of the gallery railing, and waited for the judge. He was dressed in the same Amish clothes he had been wearing at the time of his arrest, worn denim trousers, a plain blue blouse, and a blue denim vest. Behind him in the gallery, his parents sat with Cal Troyer and Vesta Miller.

"Do they have to be here?" Crist asked his lawyer. "Do they have to see me here?"

Hart sighed and wished again that Burkholder were taking greater interest in her motion to suppress his confession. "Crist," she said, sounding weary, "you need to focus on what is going to happen here."

Crist hung his head. "I don't want them to see me like this. Can't we do this someplace private?"

"We're in court, Crist. They have a right to be here."

Sheriff Robertson appeared at a side door and took one of the seats where a jury would sit. Then Judge Knowles entered through a door to the left of his bench, and the bailiff announced the judge and called Burkholder's case number.

Hart guided Burkholder to his feet while the judge was seated, and then she sat him back down, saying, "Knowles has been on the bench for thirty years."

"What?" Burkholder asked.

"He's not a rookie, Crist. That's good for us."

Knowles took up papers from his bench and asked, "Is this Mr. Burkholder, Ms. Hart?"

"Crist Burkholder, Your Honor."

Turning toward the prosecutor's table, Knowles asked, "Am I right that you oppose the motion, Ben?"

"We do, Your Honor."

Knowles nodded and asked Hart, "Does defense have any arguments beyond what is presented in this brief?"

"No, Your Honor," Hart said, standing. "The motion is complete, as you have it."

"Does the prosecutor have anything new?" Knowles asked, studying Hart's document.

The prosecutor stood and said, "Your Honor, we consider the arguments to be weak, in as much as they make assumptions about some nebulous Amish dis-awareness of legal matters. We consider that the sheriff can't be expected to take such finely divided cultural differences into consideration every time he makes an arrest."

Knowles responded, "But, under *Thompkins,* the Supreme Court has just this year ruled that a suspect must make a positive declaration in order to invoke the protections under Miranda."

Stepping forward, Hart said, "If I may, Your Honor, defense argues that even if Miranda were to have been acknowledged by the defendant, he could not have appreciated its full implications. He wouldn't have understood it sufficiently, Your Honor."

"Noted," Knowles said. He studied the papers in front of him for a moment longer, and then he looked up to say, "At some considerable length, I have studied defense's motion to suppress, and I have studied the recent *Thompkins* rulings. Accordingly, I have concluded that I am required to take into consideration the fact that the defendant is Amish. And on the narrow question of Miranda, it can be anticipated that the defendant had poor knowledge of legal matters at the time of his confession, and that he had an insufficient understanding of Miranda at the time of his subsequent questioning."

Hearing that, Robertson slipped out through the side door, wearing disappointment in all of his features.

The judge continued without taking note of the sheriff's departure. "I've considered that the sheriff and his deputies knew this at the time the defendant approached them. I've considered the fact that the sheriff did expect a confession to be forthcoming, because of his prior phone conversation with the defendant's bishop. I therefore rule in favor of defense's motion. The confession is therefore suppressed, as are all subsequent utterances of the defendant while in custody."

Burkholder stood and asked, "What does that mean, Judge?"

"Your lawyer will explain it to you," Knowles said, standing.

Hart pulled on Burkholder's sleeve and sat him down. "It means they can't charge you with murder," she whispered.

As the judge turned to exit his courtroom, Burkholder stood again and said, "I knew my rights, Judge. They didn't have to tell me about my rights. I'm guilty. I killed him. I wish to plead guilty."

"Your Honor!" Linda Hart shouted, as she rose again.

"Mr. Burkholder," the judge said, "I advise you to sit down and be quiet. There are to be no charges filed against you now."

"Judge," Crist said, "I don't want an attorney anymore. I killed Glenn Spiegle with my fist."

Immediately, Hart asked to approach the bench, and Knowles waved her forward. The prosecutor came forward, too, and Knowles covered his microphone with his palm, and scolded Hart, "Don't you have any control over your client, Ms. Hart?"

"I apologize, Your Honor. I'm as surprised as you are."

"Has your client said things like this before?" Knowles asked.

"You know I can't answer that, Your Honor."

The prosecutor argued, "Judge Knowles, you can't release him, now."

"I apologize, Your Honor," Hart broke in. "I did not advise my client to speak at all during this hearing. I told him to sit still and keep his mouth shut."

Knowles barked, "Then I gather that you anticipated he was capable of this sort of outburst!"

Hart said nothing.

To the prosecutor, Knowles said, "Do you have any other evidence on which to base charges?"

"It'd all be either hearsay, Your Honor, or facts that would not be definitive of guilt."

"Then he's free to go," Knowles told the attorneys. "Step back."

Once Hart had taken up a position behind her table, Crist rose again and said, "Judge, can't you understand this? I did it."

Hart groaned, dropped into her chair, and cradled her head in her hands. She fumed while thinking, and then stood and said, "In the interests of justice, Your Honor, I ask that my client be ordered to allocute fully to his crime."

The prosecutor stood stunned behind his table and considered what to say.

Knowles prodded him, asking, "Does the prosecution have an objection?"

"We do not, Your Honor."

Scowling, Knowles asked, "Mr. Burkholder, do you know what *allocution* means?"

"No, Your Honor."

"You have to say what you did. You have to tell the truth. Are you willing to do that now?"

"Yes, Your Honor."

"Recess Your Honor?" Hart sang out.

"Granted," Knowles said. "And unless you have something more for me, Ms. Hart, I'm going to allow him to speak. Bailiff, clear my courtroom."

* * *

While Hart consulted with Burkholder in a side room, Vesta Miller stood in the hallway outside Knowles's courtroom, talking with Wayne and Mary Burkholder. Cal sat with Robertson, on a bench at the other end of the hall.

"I didn't see this coming," Cal said.

"The judge's ruling?" Robertson asked.

"That, yes. But this confession, too."

"Cal, all we've ever really had in this case is an Amish lad who keeps insisting that he murdered a man."

"And you won't be able to charge him now?" Cal asked.

"Cal, if he keeps on talking like this, I won't have to."

* * *

Once his courtroom was reseated, Judge Knowles said to Hart, "I want your statement, Counselor. I want it on the record."

Hart rose slowly and spoke softly. "Your Honor, my client wishes to be '*set free* from his burden of guilt,' as he puts it. I've explained allocution to him at great length. I've explained the consequences to him. He knows he'll likely go to prison. He has accepted that. He insists on telling us what he did. He wants the opportunity to tell you why he did it.

"But I ask Your Honor to take into consideration the fact that he is Amish and that he is, if I may say so, Your Honor, completely naïve about crime, criminal justice, and punishment. I don't believe he has the faintest idea that there is a difference between murder and manslaughter. He is not familiar with the nuances of criminal intent or premeditation. He's Amish, Your Honor. One murder to him is like any other. He knows only his sin of aggression. As a pacifist, he believes that his crimes of pride and anger allowed him to kill a man, and he believes he deserves to be punished. If he goes to trial because of what he says this afternoon, I ask that the court appoint a psychiatrist to examine my client, so that we might understand the impulses that are causing him to insist on allocuting now to a crime for which he can no longer be charged.

"Finally, Your Honor, I ask that you hold any decision on this matter until next week. The unusual nature of these proceedings warrants careful, prolonged consideration by the court. Thank you, Your Honor. My client wishes to speak."

Seeming both astonished and perplexed, Judge Knowles sat behind his bench without speaking. Then, coming slowly and deliberately forward onto his elbows, and looking around the courtroom as if seeking greater clarity of thought—or some meaningful insight into the human condition—Judge Knowles said at last, "I want him sworn."

As the bailiff approached Burkholder, Crist rose and asked, "Is it my turn to speak?"

A strong rap of the judge's gavel put Crist back into his seat. "You're to be sworn, Mr. Burkholder," Knowles intoned. "You stand up there and keep your mouth shut, until I tell you that you may speak."

When the bailiff was ready, he carried a Bible over to Burkholder, held it out, and waited. Not knowing what to do, Burkholder stared at the bailiff for direction.

So the bailiff said, "Place your hand on the Bible, and repeat after me."

Crist hesitated and then slowly laid his hand flat on the Bible.

"Do you swear to tell the truth, the whole truth, and nothing but the truth, so help you God? If so, say 'I do.'"

Shaken and confused, Burkholder said, "I am not permitted to swear, Judge. I am especially not permitted to swear in God's name."

Instantly on his feet, Knowles shouted out, "Enough!" and came down the steps beside his bench to approach Burkholder's table. He unbuttoned his robe, pulled loose his tie, and dismissed the bailiff. Then Knowles demanded of Burkholder, "Are you going to tell the truth, yes or no?"

"Yes."

"Are you going to tell the whole truth, yes or no?"

"Yes."

"Do you consider these promises to be honorable and sacred, both to you and to God? Yes or no?"

"Yes."

The judge nodded with satisfaction and reclaimed his seat on the bench, saying to Burkholder, "Young man, you have the right to remain silent. Anything you say can, and will, be used against you in a court of law, I promise you that. You have the right to an attorney, but I see you already know that. At any rate, if you cannot afford your attorney, she will be provided to you free of charge. Your attorney will be available to you before you choose to speak, and she will surely advise you not to speak, but I gather that has already happened several times. Do you understand your rights as I have explained them?"

"Yes, Your Honor."

"Bailiff, I want him in the stand."

Once Burkholder was escorted to the witness stand, Knowles said, "OK, Mr. Burkholder. Tell me what you did."

"He offered me fifteen thousand dollars not to marry Vesta Miller, and it made me mad. I hit him with my fist, and he fell down. So I killed him."

Incredulously, Judge Knowles demanded, "What more?"

"Nothing, Your Honor. He fell down, and I went to tell my bishop."

Flaring heat into his neck and cheeks, Knowles demanded of Hart, "Did you know he would say this, Counselor?"

"I suspected it, Your Honor, but I am still rather surprised."

Turning to face Burkholder squarely, Knowles asked, "How many times did you hit Mr. Spiegle?"

"Once, Your Honor. As hard as I could."

Looking to his court recorder, Knowles asked, "Where is my coroner's report?"

The recorder handed a document up to Knowles, and halfway through it, he told his bailiff, "Get Missy Taggert over here. Get her over here right now."

* * *

Burkholder was escorted back to Hart's table, and he waited there beside his attorney, neither of them speaking. Judge Knowles leaned back in his chair with his hands clasped behind his head, his robe still undone in front, his tie still hanging loosely from his neck. Through the side door, Sheriff Robertson quietly reappeared. When Missy Taggert arrived in her green autopsy scrubs, the bailiff directed her to take a seat in the witness stand.

When she was seated, Knowles asked, "How many times was Glenn Spiegle hit?"

"Repeatedly, Your Honor."

"Which blow killed him, the first one, or later ones?"

"It's difficult to say which of the later ones, Your Honor, but the first blow was not fatal."

"The first blow simply knocked him out?" Knowles asked.

"I believe so, Your Honor. There is some guesswork here, but after an initial blow, Spiegle was beaten mercilessly, and during that subsequent beating, bones in his face and skull were fractured. That is clearly what ruptured his aneurysm."

"Missy, are you dead certain about this?"

"Your Honor, I am sure about what is in my report. The first blow did not kill Glenn Spiegle. I believe that he would have come around, eventually, and gotten up. But he was beaten subsequently. That's what killed him. The first blow did not kill Glenn Spiegle."

23

Thursday, October 8
4:30 P.M.

"HE COULD be lying," Robertson said to Cal.

"I'm sure you don't really think that," Cal said. "Just like I'm sure you never really believed this was a simple case."

They were standing outside, at the top of the steps, on the east side of the courthouse. Wayne and Mary Burkholder waited below, beside their buggy, hoping to speak with Crist, and Vesta was still inside the courthouse with Linda Hart and Crist.

"If he's not lying, Cal, then someone else found Spiegle in that barn, and beat him to death, after Crist left."

"OK," Cal said, "but who? Who hated Spiegle so much that he'd crush his skull with his fists?"

"Darba's a strong woman," Robertson offered.

"Oh, come on, Bruce. You don't believe that."

"Then maybe Billy Winters," Robertson said.

"He's in Florida, Bruce."

"Everybody *thinks* he's in Florida. What if he isn't?"

"Billy was Glenn Spiegle's best friend," Cal said. "Why would he kill him?"

"I'm just saying it's possible."

"You're grasping at straws, Sheriff."

Robertson sighed. "I know. We wasted too much time with Burkholder. Now, whoever did this is long gone."

"Unless he's local."

"What about Vesta Miller's father?" Robertson asked. "Maybe he killed Spiegle."

Cal smiled. "Sheriff, you're back to thinking that Amish people are capable of murder. That was your mistake all along."

Robertson groaned. "We made a lot of mistakes."

"Like what?"

"I should have interviewed Jacob Miller, yesterday."

"Again, Bruce, Amish aren't murderers."

"And I should have questioned Darba Winters."

"She's been worried about Billy," Cal said. "Even her psychiatrist isn't getting coherent talk from Darba right now."

"That's because she's thinking Billy isn't missing. She's worried that he's run off. That he killed Spiegle."

Behind the sheriff, the courthouse doors opened, and as Robertson made room at the top of the steps, Linda Hart stepped outside with Crist and Vesta. Hart stopped beside Cal and Robertson, and Vesta and Crist went down to Crist's parents.

Addressing Robertson, Hart said, "I know you didn't want to charge him, Sheriff. But I thought the motion to suppress was too important to pass up."

Robertson considered the lawyer skeptically and said, "Linda, you've wanted a shot at the Miranda question for years."

Hart smiled. "I won't deny it. And this was the perfect case to use."

"Oh, you used it all right," Robertson conceded. "But it was a reckless thing to do, Hart, considering that he was facing a murder charge."

"This was the *perfect* case," Hart argued. "You just don't like it that I've tied your hands."

"Now, you listen to me," Robertson started, but Hart cut him off, saying, "Don't you try to bully me, Bruce Robertson. You're an old, washed-up misogynist, whose best days are past and gone, and because of today, you won't be able to bully any more Amish folk with your ham-handed style."

"You need to simmer down, Hart," Robertson said. "You won your motion. Let it go."

"I'll *simmer down* when I'm good and ready," Hart sang. "In the meantime, you can schedule some clinics out of that big office of yours. To retrain all your deputies on Miranda."

* * *

After Hart descended the steps, Robertson watched her cross the street at the far light, and then turned to Cal and asked, "Do you think I was trying to bully her, Troyer?"

"Not you, Sheriff," Cal said, smiling.

As he spoke, Crist Burkholder climbed the stone steps and said to Robertson, "I need to get my keys back. The keys to my car."

Eyeing Cal, Robertson turned toward Burkholder and said, "You can get all of your belongings from Ellie at the front counter."

Crist hesitated, took a step down, hesitated again, and came back to ask, "The coroner really doesn't think I killed him?"

"No," Robertson said, "and really, neither do I."

After another pause, Burkholder asked, "Who would have done it, Sheriff?"

Robertson shrugged, "Someone who was very angry with Spiegle."

Cal asked Burkholder, "Was Spiegle having any trouble with anyone in the congregation?"

"Not really," Burkholder said. "Not that I knew." After thinking, he added, "Maybe Vesta's father."

"What kind of trouble?" Robertson asked.

"I wouldn't say it was *trouble,* really," Crist said. "But they argued for a couple of weeks about Vesta."

To Cal, Robertson said, "Maybe that's an angle worth considering."

Crist said, "But, two days ago, they patched it all up, and Mr. Miller told Vesta that it had all been arranged for Herr Spiegle to ask Vesta to marry him. So, that's when Vesta and I decided to elope."

Robertson asked, "Miller and Spiegle argued about Vesta, and then Miller said he'd patched it all up, so that Spiegle would agree to ask Vesta to marry him?"

"Something like that," Crist said. "Vesta says her father has been pretty happy about it these last few days."

Cal asked, "Why did Spiegle change his mind?"

"I don't know," Crist said. "We weren't going along with any of that nonsense anyway. You just can't force a girl to marry someone."

"No," Cal said. "Not in this day and age."

"What I don't get," Robertson said, "is why Jacob Miller would think Vesta would agree to an arranged marriage."

Crist shook his head. "You'd have to know Jacob Miller to understand that. He tries to control people. He told Vesta that he'd cut her out of his will if she didn't marry Herr Spiegle."

Frowning, Cal asked, "Did Bishop Shetler know anything about this?"

"I told him yesterday," Crist said. "When I was riding with him, going back to Darba Winters's place, to turn myself in."

Cal shook his head. "Leon has let this go too far."

"Jacob Miller doesn't always listen so good," Crist said. "But Vesta says that when he gets back from Florida, the bishop has instructed him to come straight to the bishop's house, instead of going home to his family."

Cal nodded a degree of satisfaction. "Sounds like Leon has had enough of this nonsense."

Crist said, "I don't think Jacob Miller is paying any attention to what the bishop thinks. He's asking for it, and you'd better believe it."

"He's gone to Florida?" Robertson asked.

Burkholder nodded. "He's made four or five trips down to Pinecraft this fall."

Robertson thought and said, "Glenn Spiegle was from Florida."

"What's the connection?" Cal asked.

"Don't know," Robertson said.

"Anyway," Burkholder said. "Vesta and I are going to leave, so I was hoping to get my car keys back."

Distracted, Robertson said, "At the front counter. See Ellie Troyer-Niell."

"Is she related to Sergeant Niell?" Crist asked.

"His wife," Robertson said. Then he asked, "How many trips to Florida?"

"Four or five," Burkholder said. "Yesterday, he flew on an airplane."

Robertson raised an eyebrow and turned to go back into the courthouse. Burkholder started down the steps, and Cal followed him, saying, "Do you need a ride out to Darba's, to get your car?"

"No," Burkholder said. "My parents will take us. I need a chance to explain to them that we can't live Amish anymore."

"Where are you going to stay?" Cal asked, descending the steps with Burkholder.

"We're going back out to Jeremiah Miller's place tonight. After we buy some new English clothes at Walmart."

24

Thursday, October 8
5:45 P.M.

CAL KNOCKED on the Brandens' door, at their brick colonial on a cul-de-sac near Millersburg College. He waited on the stoop, and then he tried the bell. After a few moments had passed, he knocked again, keyed himself in, and called out, "Caroline? Are you home?"

Getting no answer, he went down the front hallway to the kitchen, turned into the family room, and crossed to the screened back porch. There, Caroline sat in a deep wicker chair, gazing out at the eastern vistas of Amish farms. Cal stepped out onto the porch, said, "I knocked, but you didn't hear," and took a seat in a matching chair beside her.

When she turned to him, Cal saw that her eyelids were red and swollen. He touched the back of her hand, saying, "What's wrong?"

Caroline shrugged with a weak smile. "I can't stop thinking about Eddie Hunt-Myers."

Cal eased his chair closer and said, "He gave you no choice, Caroline."

"Maybe there was another way."

"He had a knife and a gun. He was going to kill us all."

"I still can't stop crying about it. Can't get the thoughts out of my head."

"And you feel guilty about it?" Cal asked.

"I feel sad, Cal," Caroline sighed, turning her eyes away. "I'm so very sad, and I can't stop crying. I get so angry, even at little things."

"That's remorse, Caroline. Good people are built to experience remorse."

"I'm not good, Cal. Not anymore. I killed a man."

"I know you're a good person, Caroline. You know it, too. You just need to learn to forgive yourself."

"I think I've forgotten how to do that, Cal, if I ever knew how. Anyway, killing Eddie washed that capacity out of me. I don't know how to get back to normal. I don't know what normal is, anymore."

"We were sheep, Caroline. He was a wolf."

"What?"

"Scripture. We are sheep among wolves. So, we are to be 'wise as serpents and harmless as doves.'"

"I can't be both, Cal. I know that, now."

"This is remorse talking," Cal said. "It's the consequence of your capacity to know guilt. So, for our own peace of mind, the scriptures teach us to be as harmless as doves. Because remorse is one of the cruelest tortures in life."

"Don't I know it!"

"So, learn again how to forgive yourself."

"It's not that simple, Cal."

Cal thought, leaned closer in his chair, and took Caroline's hand. "I just watched a lad confess repeatedly to a murder he didn't commit."

"Crist Burkholder?"

"Yes, and he needed to confess because of his intense capacity for remorse."

"He didn't kill Spiegle?"

Cal explained about the Miranda hearing and about the autopsy results that exonerated Burkholder, and he said, "So, it turns out that he didn't kill anyone. But his need to confess was so strong that he almost went to prison, trying to ease the pain of his remorse."

"But, I really did kill a man, Cal. I did it, and I can't take it back."

"I know. That's what I'm trying to explain. You can't change it, so you have to learn how to forgive yourself."

Caroline dried her eyes and gave a sad, fatalistic shrug of her shoulders. She looked around the porch to get her bearings, looked out over the backyard, and turned back to Cal to ask, "They just let him go?"

"Nobody thinks he should be held in jail."

"Did he go home?"

"No. He's taking Vesta out to Jeremiah and Sara Miller's house tonight. They'll get married and live English."

"But now he has a record," Caroline said.

"No, he was never charged," Cal said. "No record."

Caroline gave a weak laugh. "First Amish man suspected of murder, and Michael missed it all."

Cal smiled. "Now we need to figure out who really murdered Glenn Spiegle."

Caroline got up and started through the family room, toward the kitchen. "I can't get Michael out of the Duke library, Cal."

Cal followed her back into the house. "How long is this sabbatical going to last?"

"Two semesters," Caroline answered over her shoulder. "We've been down at Duke since August first."

"Why are you home?"

"I came back to manage some of the trust fund issues for his museum at the college. I should be headed back tomorrow, but I'm not done, so maybe Monday or Tuesday. Then I'm going to haul him out to the Outer Banks. Get him out of that library."

As Caroline pulled a pizza out of the freezer, Cal's cell phone rang. He answered, listened, and said, "I'll get Caroline to call him," and switched off.

Caroline turned her oven on, set the temperature, and asked, "Who was that?"

Cal shook his head. "Bruce Robertson. Jacob Miller has been killed. Down in Bradenton Beach."

Caroline stepped back from the oven. "Bruce wants me to call Michael?"

Cal nodded. "He asked if you'd call Mike, to see if he'd be willing to meet Ricky Niell down in Sarasota."

* * *

"It's all happening down in Florida, Dad," Rachel said at her computer. "Billy Winters missing, Jacob Miller shot dead, and now my truck has been seized by the DEA."

"Why?" Cal asked. "Just because they found blood in the cab?"

"No. They also found drugs hidden in the door panels. They think Billy was hauling cocaine up here, from Florida."

Sitting down beside Rachel, Cal asked, "Do you think that's possible?"

Rachel shook her head. "Not Billy, Dad. But that's his blood type, in my truck."

"How would they know his blood type?"

"I know his type," Rachel said. "All my drivers take regular blood screens, and I know all their blood types. So, it's a real big problem, Dad, that the DEA found drugs in one of my trucks."

"Is Billy still missing?"

"Yes. And Evie Carson stopped by here, about an hour ago. Darba is going nuts, worried about Billy."

"I got a call from Evie," Cal said. "While I was still over at Caroline's."

"You going out to Darba's?"

"Not until tomorrow morning," Cal said. "Evie has her sedated, tonight."

"Is Darba anything like Billy?"

Cal nodded. "She tends to nurse her little worries into bigger ones. And they're both conspiracy theory nuts, about government surveillance."

"Well," Rachel said, "if she's using her head for something besides a hat rack, she's got to be worried that somebody killed Billy over those drugs."

Cal sat and thought. Rachel stared at her monitor. Then she tapped the screen where Google Earth showed the parking lot at Bradenton Beach. "Billy's my best driver, Dad. Reliable. Honest. Always hits his waypoints. And if he's been hauling drugs, what about the rest of my drivers?"

"Billy's a good man," Cal said. "Maybe he isn't involved in any of this."

"Didn't he used to be a drunk?" Rachel asked. "It doesn't seem like him, now, but didn't he used to be?"

"A long time ago. He was drying out at a rehab clinic where Darba was a volunteer—back when she was still teaching—and she helped him get sober."

"They got married after that?"

"Many years ago. Darba didn't have any mental struggles, then. She was the best teacher, too. Loved her kids."

"They say she went a little nuts in her classroom," Rachel led.

"She did," Cal said, remembering. "She had to quit teaching, but Billy stood by her."

Rachel smiled. "They stuck together through the rough years."

Cal nodded. "Darba isn't always 'troubled.' She has her spells. But most of the time, she is fine. And the Amish kids out there all love her."

"Because of her Rum Room?"

"That, yes, but she takes the time to talk with them. Billy does, too. They help the kids figure out what they should do with their lives. You know—Amish or English—how they're going to live."

"That's just the thing, Dad. Billy can't be hauling drugs. It's just not in his nature to be doing that."

Cal nodded and looked up to study the monitor. "Will the DEA keep that truck of yours?"

"They will, if they can prove Billy was running drugs in it."

Cal shook his head.

Rachel said, "Tomorrow, when I get to work, I expect there'll be DEA agents crawling all over the place. We won't be able to ship any product until this is all cleared up."

"Is this all connected?" Cal asked. "Spiegle was from the Sarasota area."

"I don't know," Rachel sighed. "You've got Spiegle and Miller, both dead. And Billy Winters missing, with drugs hidden in his truck. My guess is that there's something that connects it all together. It just can't be Billy, is all I'm saying."

Cal got up and walked back into the kitchen, and Rachel followed him, asking, "You want some dinner?"

Sitting at the table, Cal said, "I was going to have pizza at Caroline's, but then Bruce Robertson called. Wanted me to call Mike Branden."

"Did you?"

"Yeah. He's getting on an airplane tomorrow morning, to meet Ricky Niell in the Tampa airport."

"Why isn't Robertson going himself?"

"Won't fly," Cal said, smiling.

"You're kidding."

"No. Bruce Robertson won't get on an airplane."

"Why?"

"Don't know. He's just not an airplane kind of guy. Not these days, anyway."

Rachel rolled her yellow platform over to the refrigerator, climbed up and pulled a pizza out of the freezer, and stepped down. "Could you make yourself scarce, Dad? After dinner?"

"Sure, but why?"

"I've got my first session with the sheriff tonight. He sounded pretty nervous on the phone, so I thought I'd play some of my Jimmy Buffett songs in the background, to calm him down."

"And you don't want me here to spoil the mood?"

"Under the circumstances, Dad, I don't think you'd be able to leave us alone."

25

Friday, October 9
8:35 A.M.

RICKY NIELL met Michael Branden at Tampa International Airport with a rental car. They crossed Old Tampa Bay to Saint Petersburg and then drove over Tampa Bay on the Sunshine Skyway Bridge, the long, arching span's yellow cables cresting high into a deep blue sky. Ricky wore his sheriff's department uniform, neat and trim as usual, all of the creases pressed and straight. Branden was in jeans, a yellow golf shirt, and a brown blazer, his graying beard set off by a deep tan.

As they came down off the high point of the Skyway, Ricky remarked from behind the wheel, "Cal said you've been in a library for a month, but you don't look so pale to me."

"There's lots of sun in North Carolina," Branden laughed. "Even if you're out for just an hour a day."

"You writing a book, or something?"

"Something like that. It's a new biography of Sherman."

Ricky rolled his eyes. "Don't get Robertson started on that. We'll never hear the end of it."

On U.S. 41, they turned south into Bradenton, crossing through the busy city on State Route 684, and turning west to the point at the little trailer park in Cortez. Once they had passed over the northernmost reaches of Sarasota Bay on the low Cortez drawbridge, they turned left at the light on Gulf Coast Drive and then, after three short blocks, left again, to circle back into the sleepy little community of Bradenton Beach. The police station sat next to the bridge, with a marina on the water behind it, and a white-planked fishing pier jutting out into the crystal green water of the bay. The color of light butterscotch, the two-story stucco police building hunkered in the sun on a blazing white patch of sand and crushed shells. Parked next to it was a thirty-foot aluminum police skiff on a trailer, two large outboard motors hanging off the stern. Two cruisers were parked out front, and a beach patrol officer's bicycle was chained to a steel rack beside steps and a wheelchair ramp leading up to the entrance on the second level.

They climbed the steps and entered a vestibule with a glass partition in front of a dispatcher's console. When they had rung in, a middle-aged man in khaki slacks and a tan golf shirt came into the dispatcher's room, keyed the intercom, and asked, "Business?" pointing to Niell's uniform.

Ricky said, "Holmes County Sheriff, Ohio," and displayed his badge.

The dispatcher wrote down Niell's badge number and pushed a button to release the lock on the door into the department's offices. Once they were inside, in a narrow air-conditioned hallway with offices to either side, the dispatcher introduced himself, offering his hand and saying, "Ed Vickers. The chief's not in right now."

Ricky said, "Rachel Ramsayer from Holmes County has been talking with Sergeant Raleigh Orton. So has our Sheriff Robertson."

Vickers nodded. "We call him Ray Lee. Ray Lee Orton. This about the Stevens Clark shooting?"

"Well, yes," Ricky said. "But we're interested in the man who was killed in the attack. Jacob Miller, an Amish man from Holmes County, Ohio."

Seeming to take his first note of the professor, Vickers stuck out his hand and asked, "You with the sheriff's department, too?"

Branden nodded. "Reserve deputy. Mike Branden. I help out from time to time, but mostly I teach Civil War history at Millersburg College."

"Seems like a curious mix," Vickers offered. "Professor and reserve deputy."

"I suppose it does," Branden said. "You handled the shooting? Dispatching?"

Vickers nodded. "What a mess. It happened right over there, on the bridge road. You can see it from here, if you stand outside. Anyways, a family out for a walk on the beach saw it all, and when the dad called 911, the kids were all screaming in the background of the call."

As he spoke, a policeman in a uniform shirt and bicycle shorts came up the end staircase into the hallway, and Vickers said, "Here's Ray Lee now." Vickers called Orton over and introduced the men, saying first, "Sergeant Raleigh 'Ray Lee' Orton," and then as they shook hands, "Sergeant Ricky Niell and Professor Mike Branden."

Orton noted Niell's uniform and asked, "Where are you from?"

"Holmes County, Ohio," Ricky said.

"Then I'll bet you're here because of that Amish man who was killed."

"Right," Ricky said. "And we have another murder up home. Another Amish man, Glenn Spiegle."

"You're kidding!" Orton barked out.

"No," Ricky said, surprised. "You knew him?"

"He skipped out on his parole a couple of years ago," Orton said. "We all thought he had been murdered down here, and his body disposed of."

"Why?" Branden asked.

Orton turned to Vickers. "Ed, this Ohio case is gonna connect up with Old Connie." Then to Niell and Branden, Orton said, "Let me show you something," and he led them through the outside door.

They followed Sergeant Orton out onto the parking lot in front of the police building. Orton was muscular, but also lean, thick in the chest and arms, narrow at the hips. As he led them along the Cortez Road at the base of the long bridge, Branden asked, "Does riding bicycle patrol keep you so fit, Sergeant Orton?"

Orton laughed back over his shoulder and led on, saying, "It's probably the kite surfing."

Trailing, Ricky asked, "Where are we going?"

"Two short blocks," Orton said. "I want to show you three things, and we can stand in one spot to do it."

Ricky glanced sideways at the professor, but he followed Orton down the sidewalk shaded by old cypress trees, with tall palm trees lining the other side of the road. After one short block, they had reached the sand-blown intersection at busy Gulf Coast Drive, where a continuous parade of tourist beach traffic motored up and down beside the sand of Bradenton beach itself, the waters of the Gulf of Mexico easily visible over the barrier sand, with slender grasses waving in the cool Gulf breeze.

Standing at the corner, Orton pointed out the signal lights at the intersection of State Route 684 and Gulf Coast Drive. Then, as impatient drivers made their turns from the bridge road onto Gulf Coast Drive, some heading north onto Anna Maria Island and some south along the water toward Longboat Key, Orton pointed out the left-turn lane onto Gulf Coast Drive and said, "Right here is where your Jacob Miller was killed."

Ricky produced a small digital camera and took several pictures of the intersection, saying, "We understand that he died instantly."

"Twelve-gauge shotgun, at very close range. Took the whole side of his head off."

"How'd you ID him?" Branden asked.

"Airplane ticket in his pants pocket. He didn't have a wallet. Just a roll of bills."

"You would have responded," Ricky said. "You're just around the corner."

"We got here in less than a minute, Sergeant Niell."

"Please, it's just Ricky."

"OK. Well, your Miller was in the passenger seat of an old pickup truck. They were waiting at the light, to turn left onto Gulf Coast, and he was shot by the driver who pulled up right beside them, in the right-turn lane."

"Point blank range?" Branden asked.

"Right," Orton said. "His driver—an old guy named Stevens Clark—was lucky, if you can call it that. Got clipped in the side of his face by six or seven pellets that blew past Miller's head."

"But did Clark make it?" Ricky asked.

"Yes. He's in Manatee Memorial, over in Bradenton. Came out of his second plastic surgery early this morning. He was sedated before that, so we haven't been able to talk to him much."

"But did he see who shot them?" Branden asked.

"Oh, we know who did it," Orton said, with satisfaction. "Clark recognized him when he first pulled up beside them. He told the paramedics, before they sedated him."

"Has the shooter been arrested?" Ricky asked.

Orton shook his head. "There's two more things I want you to see."

They followed Orton, crossing over to the traffic island in the middle of the intersection and on to the far side, and circled around through beach sand behind a peach-colored house set near the water's edge. Off to the north side of the house, directly in line with the T-intersection the bridge road made with Gulf Coast Drive, stuck in the sand some thirty yards back from the pavement, was a wooden cross painted white, draped with a garland of fresh roses that had been tied to the cross with white ribbon. Hand-painted on the cross, in red capital letters, was the name Ginny Lynn.

Orton toed the side of the cross gently and said, "Conrad Render pays to have a new one of these set every two months or so, and he pays a florist to bring fresh roses every day. He's been doing that for just over twenty years, since the day Glenn Spiegle killed his teenaged daughter at this intersection. And right there, just half a block south of where we crossed over Gulf Coast, in that parking lot beside the Beach House Restaurant, is where we found Billy Winters's abandoned truck."

"So, this is where Billy always parked to watch the sunsets," Ricky said.

"Right," Orton said with obvious satisfaction. "And right here is where Jacob Miller was shot. Everything happened right here, going back over twenty years."

Studying the intersection again, Branden asked, "Do you know why Winters always parked here?"

Orton nodded yes and said, "Because Billy Winters was with Glenn Spiegle the night he killed Ginny Lynn Render. They were both drunk as skunks, and they ran her over at this light. T-boned her little car and cartwheeled it forty yards out onto the sand, where it caught fire and burned."

* * *

Back at the police station, in the conference room on the lower level, Orton poured three Styrofoam cups of coffee and pulled up a chair across from Niell and Branden. But as soon as he sat down, there was a shout from the booking room at the front end of the building, and Orton pushed up from the table with a groan and went out to help.

Through the open door, Niell and Branden saw a drunk with a serious sunburn take a swing at the booking officer. Orton helped wrestle the angry man into a set of cuffs chained to the wall. The drunk punched the wall and sucked blood off his knuckles, so Orton pulled the chains tighter, and the man settled down and sat still on the bench.

Once Orton was seated again in the conference room, he said, "We have to cuff the angry drunks to the wall. To keep them from hurting themselves. Or punching one of us."

Ricky sipped his coffee and said, "We get some of that in Holmes County. Not sunburns like that one, though."

"Anyway," Orton said, "I'm surprised Spiegle lasted as long as he did. But all we knew is that he spent one day in town after he was released, and then he disappeared."

"Did anyone look for him?" Branden asked.

"His parole officer, I suppose," Orton said. "But, you've gotta figure that he was just one more guy who skipped out on his parole."

Ricky asked, "Did anyone pick up Render, to question him about Spiegle's disappearance?"

"Sure, but he denied that he did anything to Spiegle."

"He wasn't dead," Branden observed. "So, no one could have found a body."

Orton smiled. "Conrad Render is an Old Salt. He's fond of knives, and he keeps a couple of fish camps back up the Manatee River. If he had gotten to Spiegle, he would have taken him up there, and he would have made sure Spiegle took a very long time to die. Then he would have fed him to the gators, so we never really did expect to find a body. Spiegle just disappeared, and everybody figured Old Connie had made good on his promise to kill him."

The drunk in the booking room started shouting obscenities, so Orton got up and closed the door. Sitting back down, he said, "Conrad Render is the worst sort of scum you could meet. He runs drugs into shore, on go-fast boats. Keeps low to the water and travels only at night. We've never caught him with any drugs, and with those go-fast boats, he can outrun anything the Coast Guard has on the water."

Branden asked, "Are those go-fast boats like what we call cigarette boats?"

"They're long, low, and fast. Make a racket in the water, when they're out there rippin' it up. We got him cornered once, at one of the passes, but he'd already off-loaded whatever cargo he was hauling. Out in open water, he can outrun anything but a helicopter. Go-fast boats, cigarette boats, I think they're the same. And unless you deploy a fleet to box him in, you're never going to catch Old Connie out on the water."

Ricky thought, drumming his fingers on the table. "Do you think it was this Render who attacked Billy Winters?"

"That makes sense," Orton said. "But then, he could have killed Billy any week he wanted."

"So," Branden said, "maybe they were running drugs together."

"But why kill him now?" Ricky asked.

"Don't know," Orton said. "But I'll tell you this. If Conrad Render went after Billy Winters, we'd never find his body."

"Are you going to hunt him down, now?" Ricky asked. "For killing Jacob Miller?"

"It'll be the sheriff who tries for him," Orton said. "The Manatee County sheriff. About all we can do here in Bradenton Beach is put out an arrest warrant, and wait for him to get taken down on some other matter."

"But," Ricky asked, "you won't go out looking?"

Orton laughed. "There has to be about a thousand miles of river to search. And Old Connie knows it all better than anyone else. So, the chances of finding him are pretty slim."

Branden said, "We still don't know who killed Glenn Spiegle."

Orton laughed again. "I'd put my money on Conrad Render. For all three of them. Billy Winters, Glenn Spiegle, and Jacob Miller. It's the kind of play Render would make."

"OK," Ricky said. "He killed Spiegle and Winters because of his daughter. But why kill Miller?"

"Can't say," Orton said. "But you can be sure about Spiegle and Winters."

"That would mean," Branden said, "that Render found out where Spiegle had gone. So, how'd he find him all the way up in Ohio, hiding out with the Amish? Spiegle wouldn't even need a driver's license in Ohio, if he wanted to hide there. You know, disappear."

"Jacob Miller is the only connection I know of," Orton said. "He was staying with a Mennonite lady, over in Sarasota's Pinecraft."

"How do you know that?" Ricky asked.

"He wrote her phone number in the margin of his plane ticket. We called her—a Mrs. William Laver—and she said he had made half a dozen trips down here, over the last year or so."

"We should go talk to her," Branden said.

Orton got up, saying, "I'll get you a map."

Niell and Branden followed Orton up the stairs, and Ricky said, "I think we should talk to the driver, too."

"Stevens Clark," Orton said over his shoulder. "He's in Bradenton's Manatee Memorial. Maybe he can tell you what Miller was doing to get himself shot."

Orton went into one of the first-floor offices and pulled a folded map out of a desk drawer. When he handed it to Niell back in the hallway, the professor asked, "Is there somewhere else that Miller might typically have gone? You know, a place where Amish people from Pinecraft like to gather? Or a favorite restaurant or beach?"

Orton smiled. "You're going to be driving right past the north end of Lido Beach, and you ought to stop there and look around before you go see this Mrs. Laver. It's right on the county's bus route, and the kids from Pinecraft ride the bus to go swim in the ocean. I think you'll find it interesting."

"Do you think our Miller would have gone there?" Branden asked.

"No," Orton smiled, "but you ought to get a feeling for how Amish live in Florida before you talk to Mrs. Laver. It'll help you understand the Pinecraft community better."

"Is it just the kids who swim at Lido Beach," Niell asked, "or adults, too?"

"Mostly kids. The older people ride farther, to the park at South Lido Beach. There's a lot of trees there, and they have picnics in the shade."

Niell shook his head and smiled. "This isn't anything like what we know about the Amish up in Ohio."

"That's my point," Orton said. "If Jacob Miller stayed with Mrs. Laver in Pinecraft, nobody would have thought it was unusual that he was out running around from time to time. On those county buses, the Amish can go just about anywhere. Lido Beach, Siesta Key, even up here to Bradenton Beach and Coquina Beach. And if they don't want to wait for a bus, they rent a van and hire a driver to take them to the malls or to Walmart. So, Jacob Miller would have fit right in with the Amish community at Pinecraft. They get around quite handily, all over the Sarasota/Bradenton area, even though none of them owns a car."

26

Friday October 9
11:30 A.M.

CAL PULLED his truck into Darba's drive under a gray overhang of clouds, and before he had switched the engine off, his cell phone rang. He put the truck into park, checked the display, answered the call, and said, "Hi, Mike. You in Florida yet?"

"Bradenton Beach," Branden said. "We just talked to the cop that Rachel has been talking with."

Branden was standing on the concrete steps at the top level of the police station, waiting for Ricky to retrieve the car from a side lot and turn it around on the narrow, sandy street in front of the building. While he waited, he told Cal what they had learned about Conrad Render's murdering Jacob Miller, and about Spiegle's driving drunk with Billy Winters, causing the death of Ginny Lynn Render.

Cal listened and then asked, "Is there anything in that saga that I can tell Jacob Miller's family? Something to ease their pain?"

"He was shot, Cal. Close range, with a twelve-gauge shotgun, and we don't yet know why. I'm not sure they need to know the details, right now. Maybe it's enough for them to know that he was murdered, and save the details until later, once we know more about motive."

"Leon Shetler is over with the Millers. I can let him decide what to tell them."

"OK. Your call."

"How do they know who shot him?" Cal asked.

Branden explained about Stevens Clark's identifying Conrad Render as the shooter, and then he said, "But I was wondering. Why would Jacob Miller have been mixed up with this Conrad Render in the first place?"

Cal switched his engine off and climbed out of the warm truck into cold October air. "We can figure Render would have wanted Spiegle dead. Maybe even Billy Winters. But I couldn't say about Jacob Miller."

"OK, but there should be records of Conrad Render's traveling to Ohio to hunt for Spiegle. And what if he made several trips before he found him?"

"That still wouldn't tell us why Jacob Miller was mixed up in any of this."

"No."

Cal thought. "Maybe this is related to why Jacob Miller was so confident he could get Spiegle to marry Vesta."

"You going to talk to her?"

"After I check on Darba."

"Caroline said she's down at Jeremiah Miller's place," Branden said.

"I'll drive down there this afternoon."

"This could be hardest on Vesta, Cal, if she wasn't getting along with her father."

"I know, but maybe she or Crist Burkholder can tell us why her father would be mixed up with your Render guy."

Branden started down the steps to Ricky's car. "Is Leon Shetler going to be able to help Miller's family, so you can go talk with Vesta? Or do you need to help Shetler at the Millers?"

"I think I should talk with Vesta. Let him work with the family."

"OK, Cal. Maybe he can learn something that we can use, trying to figure out why Render killed Miller. And Billy Winters."

"Where are you going now?" Cal asked.

"Pinecraft. I want to see if anyone there can tell us why Miller made so many trips down here."

Standing out under a gray canopy of clouds, Cal said, "Maybe Rachel can help us figure out how many trips he made to Florida."

"Wouldn't his wife know that?"

"Jacob Miller was not the kind of man to explain himself to women."

"Caroline told me he was abusive."

"I'm sure he was."

"What could Rachel do?"

"Check on bus tickets. See how many trips Miller made. See how long he stayed."

"The last time, Cal, he came down here on an airplane."

"Maybe Rachel can find out if he flew any other times. Or find out where he stayed."

"He stayed with a Mrs. Laver. In Pinecraft."

"You're ahead of me."

"He had a phone number written on his plane ticket."

After a pause, Cal asked, "You really going to Pinecraft?"

"Yes, why?"

"I always wanted to visit there. It has got to be quite some place."

"It's just Amish and Mennonite, right?"

"Yeah, Mike. Amish who go to the Florida beaches for winter. Lots of Holmes County Amish do that, and maybe that's all that was involved here with Miller."

"Now you're getting ahead of me, Cal."

"Point is, maybe that's all Jacob Miller was doing. Falling in love with Florida."

"Not if he got shot by the same man who wanted Spiegle dead."

"No, I guess not," Cal said.

"You going to tell Darba about Billy?"

"Are you sure he's dead?"

"The cop down here is sure," Branden said.

"I'll tell her once Evie Carson gets here, Mike. I can't risk it before then."

* * *

While he was still out front at Darba's house, Cal called Rachel on her cell, and she answered after one ring, with a curt, "What?"

Surprised, Cal asked, "What's all that frustration, young lady?"

"Sorry, Dad. Busy, is all. Thought you were someone calling from work. Didn't check my display."

"You're not at work?"

"I'm back home, Dad. My office is crawling with DEA agents, and they've locked me out."

"So, you were right about them."

"Of course. They're impounding all of my computers. Boxing up all my papers. It's the same all over the office."

"So, you probably don't have much to do," Cal said, intending it to be lighthearted.

"I've got more, Dad! I've got to do everything from home, with no files. No documents. No resources. And I've got a payroll coming up."

"OK, OK. I just thought maybe you could work on something for me. But maybe it can wait."

"What is it?" Rachel asked, calmer. "Maybe I can fit it in."

"Are you sure?"

"Just tell me, Dad. I'll help if I can."

"OK, well, I need travel itineraries. For Jacob Miller, going down to Pinecraft on the Pioneer Trails buses. We need to know about all of his trips, going back maybe a year."

"How would I go about doing that, Dad?"

"I thought maybe you could 'hack into' something. Maybe hack the bus company records. Airlines, too."

"I can't just 'hack into' stuff, Dad."

"I thought that was the type of thing you could do."

"Oh, it is. But, it might get us both into more trouble than it would be worth. Especially with the DEA watching every move I make."

"Oh."

"Why don't you just call the bus company? Ask them straight up?"

"Well, I need to check on Darba, right now," Cal said. "Then I need to go see Vesta."

"This for the sheriff's office?"

"Well, yes. Ricky Niell and Mike Branden need to know. They're down in Florida."

After a pause, Rachel said, "Let me see what I can do."

"Maybe I'll just ask Bruce Robertson," Cal said.

"What's he gonna do, Dad? With Ricky down in Florida, he's got to be stretched pretty thin on deputies."

"Well, that's sort of my problem, really."

"I'll ask him," Rachel said. "He's coming here for a lunchtime lesson, anyway, and if what you need is really the sheriff's business, maybe he can clear it for me to do the search."

Smiling, Cal said, "Maybe while you've got him there, you could teach him how to hack into something."

"That's not what I do, Dad."

27

Friday, October 9
12:00 noon

RICKY DROVE the professor south out of Bradenton Beach on Gulf Coast Drive, skirting the beaches to their right, falling in with the slow tourist traffic, as drivers watched for the rare parking spot to open up along the sandy berm. After they passed the tall trees lining the picnic grounds at Coquina Beach, traffic sped up, and they soon had crossed the drawbridge over Longboat Pass, with sailboats on the luminous green waters of the Gulf to their right, white sails bright against a sky so blue that it seemed improbable to men from the gray north of Ohio.

On Longboat Key, they passed fenced properties where sprawling coastal mansions anchored the sand, with front-facing views of the Gulf waters. Farther south, they could see taller condominium buildings and towering hotels fronted by wide expanses of lawn and stands of palms, many of the distant buildings done in pastel colors, most sporting bright orange, quarter-round ceramic roofing tiles. Once they had driven over New Pass, with water so green that it seemed to be lit for effect from below, they entered the traffic circle in St. Armands and curved around counterclockwise, passing elegant shops painted in bright, tropical colors. The streets were thick with pedestrian shoppers in summer attire, strolling among shops accented with flowering shrubs and clusters of classical white statues, most of them copies of originals from Italy or France.

They had driven three-fourths of the way around the circle before realizing they had missed the turnoff for Lido Beach, so they continued around the circle and angled off toward the west once they had gotten back to the right spot. After two city blocks lined with expensive homes, they reached the sand dunes at the Gulf Coast and followed the street as it curved toward the south, skirting Lido Beach to their right.

Tall condominiums and hotels stood on the beach properties ahead, but before they reached them, a parking lot appeared on the right, and Niell pulled in and found a rare free spot at the back of the lot. The two men got out of the car. Branden laid his sport coat on the seat and Niell locked up. They crossed the sandy parking lot to wooden steps and an arched boardwalk that led over the dunes toward the water.

The white sand of Lido Beach stretched for fifty yards down to green water. It extended both to their left and to their right along an arching coastline of several miles, dotted with bright beach umbrellas in a variety of colors stuck in the sand, like a strand of jewels strung along the water's edge. To the north, the coastline eventually turned in at New Pass, at the top of Lido Key, and to the south, the arch of white sand and green surf led the eyes into the distance, where tall hotels on Siesta Key shimmered behind a hazy spray of wind-blown surf and sand, like a border of white marble monuments separating emerald water from ultramarine sky.

On the beach in front of the men, there were easily a thousand vacationers lying out either in the sun or in the shade of their umbrellas. Nearly as many swimmers played in a light surf as a gentle rhythm of low waves broke slowly as soft foam on the sand. Niell and Branden stood at the end of the wooden walkway, both somewhat taken aback by the colorful spectacle of sun-bleached ease displayed before them, their northern Ohio biorhythms—braced for the oncoming winter back home—clashing with the scene before them.

Eventually, Branden asked, "Should we walk along the water and see if we spot any Amish kids?" but as he spoke, a young Amish woman in a long gray dress and black bonnet came over the boardwalk behind them and started across the sand toward the water, carrying a basket and a small red and white cooler with the Pepsi logo. When she had threaded her way between the sun umbrellas and the many people stretched out on the sand, she spread a towel from her basket beside two other beach towels at the high-tide line and sat down facing the water. Soon two younger Amish girls in two-piece bathing suits came out of the water and joined the Amish woman at the towels, where they dried themselves and sat down to put on their own bonnets, over hair that was wrapped in buns at the backs of their heads. Niell pointed beyond the surf, and there in chest-high water stood three boys with pale white shoulders and black Dutch haircuts, waving back at the girls on the beach.

Branden shaded his eyes and gazed along the stretch of white sand toward the north, and soon he was able to point Niell's attention to a young Amish couple about forty yards up the beach, standing at water's edge in traditional attire, the woman's long forest-green dress snapping in the ocean breeze, the man holding his straw hat on his head as he watched sailboats on the horizon. Taking his hat off, the man said something to his partner, and she laid her head back and laughed as if he had spun her at a dance. He spoke again, and she studied his face for a moment, and then smiling as if she shouldn't trust him, she started moving tentatively into the water, where the small waves cresting near shore stirred the hem of her dress at her ankles. The Amish man waved her farther out, and she hesitated. Again he waved her forward, and again she laughed and waded deeper into the water, until the skirt of her long green dress was swimming in the waves at her hips. Laughing as if something were tickling her, she called for him to join her, and he sat immediately to take off his boots and socks. Soon he was out with her, his denim trousers hip-deep in the ocean water, the two splashing each other like young children when the waves crested around their waists.

Branden looked at Niell, and Niell laughed, saying, "Professor, did you ever expect to see anything like that?"

Branden had no answer for the sergeant. He just scratched at his beard, shook his head, and started back toward their car. As they were opening the car doors, a SCAT bus pulled to a stop along the sidewalk bordering the parking lot, and four more Amish kids climbed down from the bus carrying towels, baskets, and coolers of their own. Branden pulled his sport coat out of the car and got in with it laid across his lap, but Niell stood beside the car to watch as the kids made their way across the parking lot to the wooden steps at the edge of the sand. Once they had disappeared over the dune, Niell said, "This Pinecraft has got to be something to see," and he got in shaking his head, waited for the professor to buckle up, and drove out of the lot.

Back in traffic at St. Armands Circle, Niell drove halfway around the circle and headed east over the high-arching John Ringling Causeway, into the stone and glass architecture of downtown Sarasota. Then they drove around the bay, south on State Route 41, passing the parade of boats at the Bayfront Marina and the modern sculptures lining the waterfront walkways. At Bahia Vista, they turned east again and followed the wide boulevard for a mile, crossing over a narrow channel past the little hand-lettered sign for Pinecraft Park. There, they entered an Amish community of summer cottages, small houses, and trailers bearing familiar Holmes County names: Helmuth, Wengerd, Yoder, Weaver, Keim, Gingerich, and Miller.

Some of the houses mixed into the closely packed neighborhood were old and relatively stately, but most seemed to be afterthoughts on the original property. Next to an old Florida bungalow with a shaded front porch, there was a twenty-by-twenty brick hut with a tired aluminum overhang and an old air conditioner propped into a small window on two-by-four posts anchored on cinder blocks in the sand.

Ricky turned at a corner with a tidy pink stucco cottage under bushy cranberry trees, and then they saw a single-wide trailer of fifties vintage, with a broad, green-roofed carport over a patch of concrete only half long enough for a car to park. Under the roof, there sat an electric-motored wheelchair with the battery connected to a charger plugged into an outlet at the side of the house. The bicycle parked on the sun-withered lawn had a wicker basket fixed over the back fender, and next to it sat a three-wheeled cart with an electric battery and motor mounted underneath the frame.

Next came a weathered wood shanty that was improbably small, and then a cottage big enough to sleep only two or three people, with three tall solitaire palms waving overhead. On the next lot, there stood an old house painted a faded lilac, with a newer cottage built close against its side, tall jacarandas sweeping their wispy leaves against the blue sky overhead. Beyond the jacarandas, three trailers were lined up side by side, and on a larger lot further into the neighborhood, five more trailers fanned out to guard a semicircle lined with saw palmettos, with a broken sidewalk leading out to the lane. Other houses in the community were newer, but they were all uniformly small. Their windows were tiny, often shaded with canvas or wood awnings, and where there were carports beside the houses, adult-sized tricycles were parked in the shade of the covers.

At the address provided by Sergeant Orton, Ricky found Mrs. Laver's single-wide trailer, three blocks south of the Pinecraft Post Office shed, on the street with the Mennonite Tourist Church. When they knocked on the door, it was answered by a silver-haired woman, wearing a plain gray dress that reached her ankles. Her hair was up in a bun, and instead of a prayer cap, she had tied a simple white cloth over her head. She wore neither jewelry nor makeup, and she greeted the two men with a simple, "Yes," studying Niell's uniform with intelligent eyes set off by a deep Florida tan.

Niell explained briefly their interest in Jacob Miller, and Mrs. Laver nodded and stepped aside to admit them into her small trailer home. She turned them left, into a living area with two soft chairs, and once they were seated, she excused herself, stepped into the kitchen area, and pulled a pitcher of iced tea out of her little refrigerator. Without asking, she poured tea into two green plastic tumblers, and brought the drinks to the men. Once they had each tasted it, she pulled a dining chair into the living area and asked, "Sugar?"

Branden answered, "No, thank you," but Ricky handed his glass back, saying, "If you don't mind."

Back in the kitchen, Mrs. Laver stirred sugar into Ricky's glass, and she carried it back to him, saying, "Jacob Miller came here nearly half a dozen times, I think. Anyway, it was something like six times, beginning September, a year ago."

Ricky sipped tea and waited. Once Mrs. Laver was seated, he asked, "Did he just sleep here, or did he take his meals here, too?"

"Oh, he just used my spare room. It's my sewing room, but he put a mattress on the floor and just slept here."

Thinking about that, she added, "The only reason he stayed here, I suppose, is that he used to know my William, and since they were friends, I let him sleep here. He said he didn't have a lot of money, but then, he did hire a private driver."

Branden asked, "Do you know what he was doing, when he came down here?"

"He was out chasing around," Mrs. Laver frowned. "Like I said, he hired a driver. He could have gone anywhere, for all I knew. Sometimes, he came back late, after I had retired."

"You gave him a key?" Ricky asked.

"Oh, we don't lock our doors, here, Deputy."

"Was he just a tourist, do you think?" Ricky led.

"Right at first, I would guess so. Yes. But the last few times he was here, he was definitely looking for someone."

"Do you know who?" Branden asked.

"The mother of a friend, was all he told me. But I gather she had died. Then, that last time, he was looking for someone else. But the only reason I know that is because he had an argument with his driver. Something about running all over Cortez and Bradenton Beach. The driver wanted better pay. Said it was going to take all day, and he had other things he could be doing."

Ricky thought. "Was he here yesterday? Or maybe the day before?"

"No."

"When was his last visit?" Branden asked.

"It was summer, this year," Mrs. Laver said. She held up a finger, rose, consulted a wall calendar, and sat back down, saying, "August tenth and eleventh."

Branden looked over to Niell. "Maybe he moved into a hotel."

"I think he did," Mrs. Laver offered. "That August eleventh, he packed his bag and told his driver to run him up to a motel in Bradenton Beach."

"Do you know how long he stayed that time?" Ricky asked.

"No, and after that time, he didn't come back here anymore."

Ricky stroked a finger over his mustache. "Up in Ohio, Mrs. Laver, Jacob Miller was not known as a very generous man."

"If you ask me," Mrs. Laver said, "he was stingy."

Smiling, Ricky asked, "Why do you say that?"

"He promised to help me with the rent, but he never gave me a dime. He ate snacks out of my refrigerator at night, too, and he never gave me a dime to help out."

Leading the conversation, Branden said, "I suppose most people who visit down here expect to help out with food or rent."

Mrs. Laver nodded. "The buses can bring anyone. So you don't always know who is coming down. Folks up north don't always give much warning. We all just ride our carts and tricycles up to the church parking lot and meet the buses whenever they come in. One day you'll have company, and the next—maybe for a week or two—you won't have anyone. But we all know each other, and whoever shows up, we find a place for them to stay."

Still interested, Branden asked, "What do people do when they get down here?"

Mrs. Laver laughed and spoke through a broad smile. "Why, they 'hit the beaches,' Professor."

"On the buses," Branden concurred. "We just saw some kids at Lido Beach."

Mrs. Laver nodded with a smile. "A whole family will go for the day. Parents, kids, grandfolks. They can ride the buses just about anywhere down here, and the first place they all want to go is Siesta or Lido. The beaches."

"Do they do anything else?" Ricky asked. "Boats, fishing, shopping?"

"Oh, we all like to window-shop. And some go over to the causeway pier to fish. But mostly they go to sit on the beach. Walk in the surf. Maybe take a dinner cruise to look at the sunset over the water."

"Then," Branden said, "it really was unusual that Jacob Miller hired a driver to take him around, privately. If he were just a tourist, like everyone else, he could have taken a bus for far less money."

Laver nodded. "Or, he could have gotten a ride somewhere in one of the vans people hire out. You know, to go to the malls. I think Jacob might have gone to the beach once, the first time he came down. After that, he went nosing around on his own. Nosing around all over the keys. Up to Bradenton Beach, even Anna Maria Island. He wasn't on a vacation. Not Jacob Miller. He was looking for someone. And his driver wasn't too happy about it, either."

28

Friday, October 9
12:15 P.M.

CAL KNOCKED on Darba's front screened door, and it was Katie Shetler who answered, dressed in plain surf turquoise, with a black bonnet on her head. She pushed the screened door open for Cal and held her finger to her lips, whispering, "Darba just fell asleep."

Cal came in and asked softly, "Is she any better?" and Katie shook her head.

They sat in upholstered rockers in the living room, and Katie said, "She was up all night, Cal. Pacing the halls. She mutters 'Billy's not dead,' like someone told her he was."

"We really don't know for sure," Cal said, "but a Sergeant Orton in Bradenton Beach thinks he was killed by the same man who killed Spiegle and Miller."

"But, why would he do all of that?" Katie asked, consternation plain on her face.

"Mike Branden explained a lot of that to me," Cal said. "He called just now, from Florida."

Cal told her what he had learned from the professor about Jacob Miller's murder, and then he said, "Glenn Spiegle was driving drunk, Katie, when he was twenty-two. Billy was riding with him, and they killed a young girl with Spiegle's car. She was only sixteen, and her father has always wanted Spiegle dead. Mike Branden figures that Spiegle was hiding from his past, up here. That he was hiding from Conrad Render."

"We thought he just wanted to live Amish," Katie said, shaking her head.

"He did, Katie. But he also knew Mr. Render would kill him, if he ever found him."

"How did he find him, Cal?"

"I don't know, but Jacob Miller has been nosing around down there, and maybe he tipped Render off. Maybe he told him, somehow, where to look for Spiegle."

"Why would he tell him that?"

"Maybe he didn't. Maybe he was just asking around about Spiegle, down in Florida, and Render caught on. Maybe Render followed Miller home one time, and figured out where Spiegle was."

Katie shook her head sadly. "How is anyone ever going to know what really happened?"

Cal said, "We're going to try to see how many times Miller went to Florida, and how many times Render came up here. Maybe there'll be a pattern in their travels."

Shrugging, Katie said, "It really doesn't matter, Cal. The harm has been done."

"No, I suppose not," Cal said. "But Bruce Robertson is going to want to solve the Spiegle murder, if he can. Solve the Miller murder, too."

"I thought you said that the professor said that they have a witness to the murder of Jacob Miller."

"They do," Cal said. "But now they want to catch the murderer."

"What good will that do?" Katie asked. "It'll just put more lives at risk."

Cal smiled. "They wouldn't just let it go, Katie."

"They would if they were wise."

There was another knock at the door, and Katie rose and opened the screened door for Evelyn Carson.

Carson came in and asked, "How is she?" She nodded at Cal.

"Sleeping," Katie said, finger to her lips to whisper.

Carson took a seat on the couch. Cal related what he knew from his conversation with Mike Branden that morning, and finished by saying, "We were hoping you could tell Darba that Billy is probably dead."

Behind them, from the long hallway back to her bedroom, they heard Darba say, assertively, "Billy's not dead."

When they stood to look back into the hallway, Darba came forward in her robe, saying, "Billy can't be dead," tears streaming her cheeks, her fingers knotting in tangles in front of her robe.

Carson stepped forward and brought Darba into the living room. Once she was seated, Darba shook her head, sluggish from the drugs, and said, "I just wanted them to have a safe place."

"What, Darba?" Carson asked. "What are you talking about?"

"My Rum Room," Darba said. "I just wanted kids like Vesta and Crist to have a safe place to go. To get away from their families for a while. To get away from Vesta's father. A safe place for Rumspringe. A place to run wild."

"It's not your fault," Carson said.

"It is," Darba muttered. "It's all my fault."

"No, Darba," Cal said. "This is Jacob Miller's fault. He's the one who pushed Vesta and Crist away."

"And Mr. Render," Katie added. "He's the one who killed Glenn Spiegle."

Darba turned her dull eyes to Katie. "Is he the one you think has killed my Billy?"

Katie turned to Cal, and Darba looked to him, too. Cal said, "Yes, Darba. We think he killed Billy."

Darba pushed up and started down the hallway toward her bedroom, pronouncing, "You just don't understand. Billy can't be dead."

* * *

Back outside, on Darba's driveway, Cal asked Katie, "Do you think Leon is going to need any help with the Millers today?"

Katie shook her head. "He has the whole church helping, Cal. They'll all be over there now, to sit with them."

"Then can I bring anything?" Cal asked. "Food, drinks, something like that?"

"We Amish know how to tend to these matters better than anyone, Cal."

"I know," Cal said, smiling. "I'll use the time to go see Vesta."

"She'll need to talk to someone," Katie agreed.

Cal opened his truck door and paused before he got in. The clouds overhead were thicker and darker than when he had arrived, with a cold breeze blowing over the hilltops. "Do you know why Jacob Miller was so confident that he could get Spiegle to propose to Vesta?"

"No, Cal," Katie said, hugging herself in the cold wind. "But, if you ask me, he shouldn't have even tried."

Cal nodded agreement. "Was he really like that? You know—thought he could boss his family like that?"

Katie nodded. "Leon was working on that. The bishop would have gotten that under control."

Cal thought, studying dark clouds that were rolling in from the west. "Are you coming back here, today?"

"Later," Katie said. "Along towards supper."

"I have a friend who could use a little company. Maybe have a talk."

"Who, Cal? Talk about what?"

"The professor's wife, Caroline. She killed a man last year, in self-defense."

"And now she's sorry?"

"Tormented by remorse is more like it," Cal said.

"I could talk to her. Maybe you could bring some pizzas."

"When should I come out? About five or six, tonight?"

Katie nodded. "And I think she should talk with the bishop. He knows a thing or two about the torment of remorse."

29

Friday, October 9
12:50 P.M.

ON MRS. Laver's recommendation, Ricky pulled into the back parking lot at Yoder's Restaurant on Bahia Vista Street and found a parking spot at the edge of some shade. Around front at the crowded door, they took a place in line to wait for a lunch table, sandwiched between a retired Amish couple ahead of them and a tourist family behind them, with three kids squabbling over two coloring books.

The line moved toward the door only slowly, and while they waited in the heat, trying to take advantage of a thin line of shade next to the building, Ricky offered the occasional speculative comment.

"Maybe Jacob Miller killed Spiegle," he said.

"Motive?" Branden asked, eyeing the line ahead for movement.

"Don't know," Ricky answered. "Maybe Miller found out why Spiegle was in Holmes County."

"And what, Ricky? Blackmailed Spiegle?"

An Amish couple came out of the restaurant, the lady carrying a take-home box, her husband picking at his teeth with a round toothpick.

"Could be," Ricky said. "He could have blackmailed him, to force him to propose to Vesta."

"She never would have married him. Spiegle had to know that."

"OK," Ricky offered, "then Miller could have demanded money from Spiegle. To keep quiet."

The line shuffled forward.

"If that were the case, why would Miller kill Spiegle?"

"Back to that," Ricky sighed. "OK, maybe Miller told Render where to find Spiegle."

"More likely," Branden said, "Render followed Miller or Billy Winters home a time or two and found Spiegle himself."

"Then Rachel should find records of those trips," Ricky said. "But a guy like Render would travel under an alias."

"True," Branden said, and Ricky nodded and opened his phone.

Ricky punched in Sergeant Orton's number, and after he had him on the phone, he asked, "Ray Lee, can you give us any aliases that Conrad Render has used in the past?"

After listening briefly, Ricky said, "OK, wait a minute," and he fished a notepad out of his uniform breast pocket. Then with Branden turned around so he could write against his back, Ricky wrote as he repeated the names, "Daniel Walters. Scuddy Hawk. Peter Williams. Bobbie Jackmann. William Jeffries. OK, thanks, Ray Lee."

* * *

As their line for lunch inched forward, Ricky called Bruce Robertson with his list of aliases for Conrad Render, and when he switched off, he said to Branden, "That's funny. The sheriff said he was 'taking a lesson' at Rachel Ramsayer's house. He said he'd have her run the aliases right then. He's gonna have her work for the sheriff's office, checking travel lists with the bus company, and with the airlines out of Akron/Canton and Cleveland."

"Why is that funny?" Branden asked. They were inside the door now, joining the press of people waiting in front of the hostess's podium.

Ricky studied the tables where people still sat with their meals. "It's funny that Bruce Robertson would be taking lessons from Rachel, is all."

"What kind of lessons?"

"Don't know."

The line moved forward as a party of six people was seated, and Ricky's phone chirped. He answered it, listened, frowned, and said, "We'll be there in thirty minutes."

As he threaded a path back through the line to the outside of the restaurant, Ricky said over his shoulder, "That was Orton. The sheriff of Manatee County is organizing a joint team with the Coast Guard, to search the fish camps that Conrad Render keeps on the Manatee River."

* * *

While Branden drove back north on Longboat Key, mumbling about missing lunch, Ricky got Orton on the phone again.

"Are we going out on a Coast Guard vessel?" Ricky asked. "They've got those UTB-41 boats, up on Lake Erie."

"They'll use those," Orton said over the phone, "but now they also have the Raider Twenty-fives. The RBS-25. They're much faster."

"We'll be on one of those?"

"No, no," Orton said. "You boys are going out with me, on our police skiff. We're putting her into the water now. You just pull in at the marina behind the station, and I'll get you suited up with life vests, because the wind is starting to chop it up, out on the bay. Can you boys swim?"

"*Yes,*" Ricky replied, insulted. "We can swim."

"Good," Orton said, taking scant note of Niell's tone. "We probably won't see any action, because we'll be bringing up the rear. And if Render is up there on the Manatee, maybe on a go-fast boat, it'll be the Coast Guard helicopters that have to chase him down."

"We wouldn't be able to keep up?" Ricky asked.

"Not even close, Sergeant. Compared to those Coast Guard boats, our skiff is like a bathtub with a motor hanging over the edge. I just thought you might like a boat ride up the river. We'll hang back and let the sheriff do the hard work. Then, if they do manage to flush Old Connie out of some hole, he'll have to come back past us."

30

Friday, October 9
2:40 P.M.

"MICHAEL," CAROLINE scolded into her phone, "you let the sheriff hunt down this Render." She was riding beside Cal in his truck, going south on State Route 83 toward the Doughty Valley, with a cold gray sprinkle of rain wetting the windshield.

"We'll just be in a police skiff," Branden said. "We're just going to be observers."

"Is Ricky driving that boat?" Caroline shot out. "Because if he is, I don't want you anywhere near it!"

"Where is this coming from?" Branden asked, surprised by her intensity.

"Last time you were on a boat with Ricky Niell," she said, "he almost got you killed."

Branden laughed, "That was over ten years ago, Caroline."

"I don't care, Michael."

"We won't be on the lead boat."

"I don't care. I don't like it."

"I'll be careful. Besides, the life vest is almost bigger than I am."

More frustrated than normal, Caroline handed the phone to Cal and said, "You talk to him."

Cal held the wheel with one hand, took the phone, and pulled to the side of the road. "Mike," he said. "You going after Render on a boat?"

Branden explained the plan to search the Manatee River fish camps, and said, "Tell her we'll hang back in the rear, Cal."

"He says he'll hang back," Cal said to Caroline.

"And you believe him?" Caroline scoffed.

"She doesn't believe you," Cal said into the phone.

"This is why we're down here, Cal. We think Conrad Render killed Glenn Spiegle. We know he killed Jacob Miller. Probably he killed Billy Winters, too."

"I know," Cal said looking to Caroline. "But you can let the sheriff down there run this search for Conrad Render, right?"

"Sure, Cal. Tell her that."

To Caroline, Cal said, "He says he'll let the sheriff down there run this search."

Caroline shouted toward the phone, "Not the lead boat, Michael! Don't you put yourself on that lead boat!"

Branden gave Cal a self-conscious laugh and said, "Tell her I'll hang back, OK, Cal?"

"Right," Cal said and switched off. He handed the phone back to Caroline and said, "He promised he'll hang back. He's not going to be on the lead boat."

Agitated, Caroline asked, "And you believe that?"

Cal pulled back onto the road. "This isn't like you," he said. "You usually don't fret over him like this."

Caroline sighed out frustration. "Everything hits me harder, these days. Everything seems so much more troublesome than it should be."

"When we're done here at Jeremiah's, I want you to go out to Darba's with me. I want you to talk with Katie Shetler. We'll try to figure out why you're so sad."

"I know why I'm sad, Cal. It's all about Eddie."

"Yes, but you can let it go. You can set the pain aside."

"I told you. I don't know how to do that."

"That's what I want you to talk to Katie about."

"OK, but first, why do you want me to talk with Vesta?"

"I thought we could both talk with her. She's going to be sad about her father, and she doesn't have the resources of her family anymore."

"She didn't really like her father, Cal."

"Yes," Cal said, "and that may make it worse for her."

* * *

Cal and Caroline knocked on the front door at Jeremiah Miller's house, but no one answered. From the barn behind the house, they heard the high scream of a power saw cutting into wood, so they stepped off the porch into the cold drizzle to follow a concrete walkway around to the back of the house. The walkway led further back to a tall, red bank barn, and on the high side of the bank, in the corner of the barn, there was a door into the top level. As Jeremiah's saw cut into the wood again, a blower at the side of the barn's top level exhausted dark sawdust through a vent pipe, onto a dark, rain-soaked cone of sawdust on the ground below. It was walnut, today, Cal thought, as he pulled the door open and smelled the wood. It was the sweet aroma of walnut, the best of the forest hardwoods.

Inside, Cal stepped up to the screened cage where Jeremiah kept his power tools and lumber. He pounded loudly on the cage door and waved to Jeremiah when he turned to look up from his saw. Pulling his earplugs out, Jeremiah switched off his saw, and then he stepped to the far wall and turned off the gasoline engine that ran his drive belts up in the rafters. He brushed the fine, black sawdust off his denim jeans and the sleeves of his blue shirt and stepped out of his workshop cage.

Jeremiah shook hands with Cal and nodded a greeting to Caroline, and Cal said, "We thought maybe Vesta would be here."

Jeremiah led them back toward the house, saying, "They'll be back soon. They all went over to Becks Mills in the buggy."

"Is Vesta doing OK?" Cal asked, as he followed Jeremiah toward the house.

Jeremiah pulled the back door open, and brought Cal and Caroline into the kitchen, where he helped them out of their raincoats. "She seems fine to me, Cal. She's not sad, if that's what you mean."

Cal looked to Caroline and back to Jeremiah. "It's going to hit her sometime, Jeremiah."

"Mostly," Jeremiah said, "I think she's sad for her family."

There came the clatter of buggy wheels and horse's hooves on the gravel of the drive outside, and Jeremiah pulled curtains aside to look out over the sink. Letting the curtain go slack, he said, "They're back."

* * *

While Jeremiah and Sara unloaded groceries in the kitchen, Crist and Vesta sat with Cal and Caroline in the front parlor. Vesta was dressed English, in a new pair of loose-fitting Levi jeans, with penny loafers on her feet and a button-front blouse with a bright orange hibiscus pattern. She had a new watch on her left wrist, a black digital Timex that still had the shiny gold price tag wrapped around the strap, and she wore a set of plastic pearls around her neck. Her hair was still up in an Amish bun, but she wore no prayer cap. As small as a woman could be and still not be thought a child, she wore a nervous pride in her new look, seeming to Caroline to be both happy for the transition she was making to the English side of life, and anxious about her new clothes.

Caroline sat across from her and said, "You look nice in your new outfit, Vesta."

Vesta smiled but glanced away, and Crist said, "We still have some shopping to do."

Vesta turned back and asked, "Is my father really dead?"

"Yes," Cal said. "He was murdered yesterday, down in Florida."

Vesta shook her head, seeming more angry than sad. "He should never have gone down there," she said and looked away again. "He should never have poked his nose into any of it."

"Into any of what?" Cal asked.

"Herr Spiegle's business," Vesta answered, eyes still averted. After a pause, she turned back to Cal and said, "He said he had found out why Herr Spiegle really came up to Ohio in the first place. He said it was going to be his big *payday.*"

"Why?" Caroline asked. "Why a big payday?"

Crist answered. “Everybody knew Herr Spiegle had a lot of cash money. And Jacob Miller wanted him to buy his land for cash. But Bishop Shetler ruled that Herr Spiegle should buy some of Mony Detweiler’s land, instead.”

Vesta cut in. “My father thought he could get Herr Spiegle to marry me. And the last time he came back from Florida, he told me that Herr Spiegle would *have* to marry me, now. And he told me I’d have to do as I was told. He said I was responsible for serving a man, raising a family, and it didn’t matter who I married. More than once, he told me it was going to be his big payday, when he got me married to the right man.”

Caroline bristled at Vesta’s words, but thought better of speaking.

Cal said to Vesta, “If you could speak to him right now, Vesta, what would you say?”

Vesta turned her eyes toward the floor and whispered, “I’d tell him how much he hurt me.”

“And if God were to speak to your father for you,” Cal said, “what would you have Him say?”

Vesta looked up and studied Cal’s eyes. She thought, measured her emotions carefully, and said, “That he was wrong. He was always so sure of himself, but he was wrong. And he hurt us all. He hurt us so much, Mr. Troyer, especially the women. But what has he done to my brothers? How much has he hurt them? That they might grow up to think like him makes me crazy.”

“Anything else, Vesta?” Cal asked. “Is there anything else you want your father to know?”

“No,” Vesta whispered. “Maybe if he could have known what harm he did, I’d like to hear him say that he’s sorry.”

Cal leaned forward on his seat and said, gently, “He’s saying that, now, Vesta. He knows what harm he did, and he’s saying that he’s sorry.”

“I don’t understand,” Vesta said. “He’s dead, so how is that possible?”

“In The Revelation,” Cal said, “it is promised that all the dead stand before God, and the things that they have done are read from the Book of Life. This is done because we each must give account for our own life."

Vesta nodded, but seemed puzzled. Cal explained himself.

"God acquaints each of us with the record kept in the Book of Life. He does it on His perfect terms, with absolute clarity and truth. And He has done this with your father, Vesta. He has shown him all the harm he did to his family, and I promise you, your father is saying that he is sorry. I know this because, once confronted with the truth of his life, he couldn't do anything else."

Vesta looked to Crist, to Caroline, and then down to her hands in her lap. Without looking up, she asked, "He really knows? Really knows how much he hurt us?"

"Yes," Cal said. "With God's perfect truth and clarity."

* * *

"I think you helped, Cal," Caroline said, riding back toward Millersburg. "But she's still probably going to be angry with her father for a very long time. She's going to be angry with him, like I'm still angry about Eddie."

Cal drove and shook his head. "Some people get so messed up."

"Don't I know it," Caroline said. "This Miller guy? Sounds like he was a monster."

Cal glanced at her sideways and said, "We'll take pizzas out to Darba's place. Katie could use the company."

"I thought you said it was me who needed the company."

"We'll be each other's company," Cal said and laughed. "We'll sit, eat some pizza, talk about life, and wait for Mike to call."

"All I know, Cal, is that he'd better not be on the lead boat."

31

Friday, October 9
3:35 P.M.

RAY LEE Orton's police skiff rode an angry chop where it was lashed against the pier. Behind it, the flags at the marina snapped at right angles to their poles. On their moorings nearby, sailboats strained at their lines, halyards slapping against aluminum masts, hulls pitching and rolling on the waves.

As Orton struggled into his life vest, the wind tore at his uniform shirt. Ricky and Branden stood ready on the dock, already vested, and shouted to be heard as they asked Ray Lee questions about the search party that was gathering in boats large and small on the bay waters in view of the Cortez drawbridge.

Orton's seemed to be the last vessel to be ready to push off, and by the time Niell and Branden were aboard and Ray Lee had his skiff pointed out into open waters, the lead Coast Guard Raider 25s were already passing under the bridge, throwing spray off their orange hulls, as they pushed for speed over the rough seas. Next, they saw the UTB-41s run under the bridge, their bows striped with the orange Coast Guard insignia, seamen standing ready at the rails or on the bows, the twin diesel inboards roaring with the strain of speed.

Last, and slower than the rest, came Orton's skiff. Holding tightly to the gunwale rails, Ricky and the professor stood aft of the wheelhouse where Orton piloted the boat. In the wheelhouse, Orton stood protected from the sun under a green bimini awning, wrestling with the wheel and the throttles.

On the open waters at the northernmost limit of Sarasota Bay, the chop was fierce, driven by a steady onshore wind, and Orton had trouble pushing his skiff forward toward the bridge. More than once, Branden glanced anxiously sideways at Niell, and more than once, Niell could muster only the most tentative of glances back toward Branden, his knuckles white on the railing, nervous tension in his fixed gaze.

Once they had passed under the Cortez Bridge, Orton found fractionally calmer waters, and as he chased the Coast Guard detachment up ahead, he mastered the chop and managed to keep the boat relatively stable. As he piloted the skiff northward into Palma Sola Bay, he occasionally pulled his headphones away to turn and shout back to Ricky about the plan to take Sarasota Pass to the Manatee, and then follow the river eastward for several kilometers to the first of Conrad Render's fish camps, on a tributary on the north bank of the Upper Manatee.

Ricky held fast to the railing as he fought the pitch and yaw of the deck under his boots. Catching his attention, Branden flexed his knees to show Ricky how to let his legs take the roll of the waves. Niell tried unsuccessfully at first to mimic the professor's stance, but then in short order he had managed it, and as they made the turn into the wide mouth of the Manatee, Ricky was getting his sea legs. He was also getting some of his color back, the professor noted, and Branden let go of the railing long enough to give Ricky a thumbs-up.

On the smoother waters of the river, Orton was able to open up his outboards to full throttle, and soon they were skimming over the water, the boat at maximum speed. Orton waved Ricky up into the wheelhouse, and Ricky handed himself forward along the railing. Beside Orton, Ricky found steady footing on the pilot's deck, and a good handhold on a port bimini post, and he stood beside the sergeant to listen to the radio traffic coming from the Coast Guard search boats. Eventually, word came over the radio that the first fish camp was deserted. The lead boats were pushing on to the second camp, and a deputy was waiting on the dock at the first camp to guide Orton farther up the river.

Orton pushed forward on his throttles, wanting all the power he could get, but the skiff had nothing more to give, so he eased back and settled the boat into a less determined pace, saying to Ricky, "No point in burning up all our gas just getting there."

After a few more minutes, on the north bank of the river, where a tributary stream joined the broader waters of the Manatee, they saw a sheriff's deputy waving from the bank. Render's first fish camp sat at the edge of the water, a ramshackle boat dock leaning into the water in front of a cabin of weathered boards, with a sunken roof and broken window glass.

Orton pulled up to the base of the dock where it was strong enough to take some weight, and the deputy scrambled over the old boards and aboard the skiff, saying, "There's nothing here. Hasn't been for years. I'm to tell you where the next camp is. It's hard to find."

The deputy stood on the bow and pushed off with a gaff, and then he climbed back to the wheelhouse as Orton swung the skiff around toward the east. Briefly, Orton introduced the three men to each other, and soon he had the skiff up to speed again. Over the roar of the outboards, the deputy shouted, "Three point seven kilometers upriver. Turn into the mangroves on the south bank. There's a narrow passage there, going back into the marshes. Water's deep enough down the middle to take our draft, but the UTBs will have to stand off."

* * *

Ray Lee took his skiff into the mangroves slowly, following a narrow passage that snaked for nearly a half kilometer back into the marshes beside the river. The path back in was not always clear, and at one point, he took a wrong turn and dead-ended in a tangle of cypress roots and reeds. But they managed to pole the skiff backward over thirty yards of muddy water, and then they continued farther into the swamplands on the correct course. When they broke into the open waters of a five-acre lake, they saw the Coast Guard and sheriff's boats pulled up on the sand at the far bank. Orton motored across the water slowly and nosed his skiff up to the sand between two of the orange RBSs, and the four men climbed over the bow railing, onto the wet sand.

At this fish camp, unlike the first, there were signs of recent use. For a radius of nearly thirty yards around a center cabin, the vegetation had recently been cleared away, and the sand in the clearing was heavily tracked with footprints and off-road tires. A weedy trail led out of the camp toward the south.

At the edge of the clearing stood tall cypress trees with a scattering of slender solitaire palms mixed in, and a crude fencing of razor wire and barbed wire was lashed to the trunks of the trees, marking the perimeter of the clearing. A little cabin sporting new roofing shingles stood beside the water, and beside the cabin there was a tidy stack of split firewood. The door of the cabin had been propped open with a broom that looked almost store-bought new, and sheriff's deputies were already carrying boxes of clothes, papers, and kitchen gear out to one of the boats.

In front of the cabin, there was a fire pit in the sand, with a spit hung over it from two tripod stands on either side, and in the ashes were the burnt tatters of blue jeans and a red flannel shirt. A deputy who was stirring through the ashes in the fire pit fished out a patch of blue fabric and the bill of a blue baseball cap. Behind the cabin, strung between the trunks of two pines, they found a tangle of wires and rope, with two sets of handcuffs suspended from the wires.

Outside the cabin, as the sheriff deputies finished loading boxes into the boats, Orton asked Niell, "Was your Billy Winters an Indians fan?"

Niell shook his head and drew his palm over his hair. "I don't know," he said, shaken. "Really, I don't know."

"If Render got to Winters," Orton said, "we'll never find a body."

Branden tried his cell phone, making a call to Bruce Robertson, but the call wouldn't go through. So he stood to study the fish camp and said to Niell, "Render's gone, Ricky. If he's back in here, somewhere, they'll never find him."

Niell asked Orton, "Do you have any other places to look?"

"This was it," Orton said. "These were our best chances to get him."

"So," Niell said, "he could be anywhere."

"We'll get him another time," Orton said. "But you boys might as well go home."

Niell turned in place and studied the camp. "This'd be an awful place to die," he said. "If Render brought Billy Winters back in here, this'd be just about the worst place he could die."

* * *

Once Sergeant Orton had them back at the docks at the Bradenton Beach marina, Branden was able to place his call to Robertson. He stood beside the water while Ricky finished up inside with Orton, and after he had told the sheriff about the unsuccessful search for Conrad Render, Robertson said, "OK, Mike, but before you come home, you'll want to check with Orton, again. I just faxed him the travel details for Jacob Miller, going down there on the bus over the last year. I also faxed the travel information for one of your Render aliases, William Jeffries. He traveled up here twice. Once two weeks ago, right after Jacob Miller had been down there."

Branden shaded his eyes from the afternoon sun and asked, "You think that's Conrad Render? William Jeffries, I mean."

"Yes," Robertson said. "We've checked this alias with the Manatee County sheriff's office. William Jeffries is Conrad Render. And we found the records for his flights to Akron/Canton, from Tampa International."

"*We found?*" Branden asked. "Who is *we?*"

"Rachel Ramsayer, Mike. I got her logged into bus company and airline records through FBI channels. Rachel can find anything with a computer."

"Why are you working . . . ?" Branden started, but Robertson cut him off, saying, "We're working on some Internet things, Mike."

"OK," Branden said tentatively. "Rachel knows computers, but what are you doing?"

"Mostly just looking over her shoulder," Robertson said. "Maybe taking a few lessons."

"And you said Render was up in Ohio two weeks ago?"

"Yes, he was," Robertson said. "But he also flew up here this last Tuesday, the day before Glenn Spiegle was murdered. Then he flew right back, around noon, the morning of the murder. He'd have been back in Sarasota by four P.M."

"Spiegle and Winters," Branden mumbled into his phone.

"What?"

"He could have killed both Spiegle and Winters, on the same day."

"I figure he did, Mike. I figure he killed them both. And they know he killed Jacob Miller down there yesterday."

"Busy fellow," Branden said.

There was a pause over the connection, and then Robertson asked, "Did you get a chance to talk to the driver who was shot with Miller?"

"No," Branden said. "Before we went looking for Render, he hadn't come around from his anesthesia."

"OK," Robertson said, "but check with Orton before you come home. Maybe they can make use of this new travel information."

32

Friday, October 9
6:10 P.M.

CAL JUMPED out of his truck in Darba's driveway and struggled to open his umbrella in a cold, slashing rain as he ran around to Caroline's passenger door. Once he had the umbrella up, Caroline pushed her door open with her foot and stepped out balancing three large pizza boxes. The wind caught the boxes and nearly upended them, and while Cal wrestled with his umbrella, Caroline clamped one hand over the top box and moved forward at a run, quickly outdistancing the cover Cal was offering. Cal followed close behind her, and they ran through the rain, along the front walkway, under silver flashes of lightning, with nearly simultaneous explosions of thunder overhead. As they ran, the rain blew at them on a fierce slant and pelted them with leaves and debris from nearby trees.

When they reached the front stoop, Katie Shetler pushed the screened door open for them, but the wind snatched the door handle from her fingers, and the screened door flew back and slapped flat against the side of the house. Cal tried to reach for it as Caroline darted inside, but the wind tore his umbrella inside out, so Cal tossed it down to the grass at the edge of the porch light, where the wind took it away into the dark. When Cal stepped inside, he pulled the screened door closed. Dripping rainwater onto the entryway tiles, he latched the screened door and closed the front door against the storm.

Caroline struggled out of her raincoat and reached for Cal's, saying, "These didn't do us much good."

Katie stood by, and when both raincoats were off, she carried them through the living room and into the kitchen, where she hung them side by side on Shaker pegs over Darba's boot tray.

Cal and Caroline followed Katie into the kitchen. Cal took a hand towel from the oven handle and gave it to Caroline. Then he took a second towel from a rack beside the stove and dried his hair. Katie took both wet towels down the hallway to Darba's bathroom and pulled two bath towels out of the hall closet. With these, Cal and Caroline were able to dry off enough to sit at the kitchen table without dripping onto the floor.

While they were sitting down with Katie, Darba shuffled into the kitchen in her blue robe and a pair of fuzzy pink bedroom slippers, and after looking at Cal and Caroline, she went back down the hall and brought a long, terry-cloth bathrobe for Caroline and a dry pair of jeans for Cal. Caroline went into the bathroom first, took off her wet blouse and jeans, and pulled on the oversized robe. While she did that, Cal asked Darba if she had a dry shirt, and Darba brought out a Cleveland Indians jersey for Cal to wear. When Caroline came out in Darba's spare robe, Cal went into the bathroom and changed into Billy's jeans and jersey. Then, once they were in dry clothes, Katie hung the wet clothes on the Shaker pegs, and Katie and Darba took seats in the living room with Cal and Caroline.

Darba sat without speaking, her gaze wandering slowly around the room. She brushed at hair hanging in front of her eyes, but to Cal, the motion seemed sluggish. He asked, "Have you been able to sleep, Darba?" and she turned her eyes slowly toward him, saying only, "A little, I guess."

Katie said, "You should lie down again, Darba. Dr. Carson wants you to sleep right now."

Darba shook her head. "I'm waiting for Billy to call," but her eyes closed almost immediately, and she fell asleep on the couch.

Katie lifted Darba's legs up onto the couch and placed pillows under Darba's head. Then she led Cal and Caroline into the kitchen, carrying the pizza boxes.

As they were sitting down, there was a soft knock on the back door, and Katie crossed the back porch to let in her husband, the bishop. Leon propped his wet umbrella open on the back porch and came into the kitchen trailing Katie, and the four friends sat together at the kitchen table, while Darba slept in the adjoining living room.

Bishop Shetler asked Cal about news from Florida, and Cal told him about the search for Jacob Miller's murderer, as they ate pizza from the boxes. Leon listened, shaking his head with sadness, and said, "This Render held vengeance in his heart for all those years. What price has he paid for that type of hate?"

Cal shook his head and said, "I've got all I can do to answer for my own sins."

"Grace," Leon said. "But for the grace."

"I know," Cal answered. "But I don't think Conrad Render is the type to ask for forgiveness."

"He will," Leon said, "when he meets his Maker."

Cal nodded without taking any satisfaction.

To Caroline, Katie said, "The Bishop,"—she tilted her head toward her husband—"has taught often about forgiveness."

Caroline blushed and looked to Cal for an explanation.

Cal said, "I told Leon and Katie that you've been struggling with remorse."

Caroline smiled self-consciously and said to the bishop, "I killed a man in self-defense. I can't shake the guilt I feel. It's tearing me apart inside."

Tears appeared in her eyes. Caroline wiped them with the flats of her fingers, and then she accepted a handkerchief from Cal and dried her eyes with it.

Katie retrieved napkins from a drawer, set them out beside the pizza boxes, and sat back down. Intending encouragement, she said to her husband, "Tell her what you tell Darba about grace, Leon."

But Caroline interrupted her, saying, "Really, I know about forgiveness. I just can't seem to find it for myself. It seems so out of reach to me, like it's parked on the moon or something. I can see it, but I can't reach it. It's—I can't think of another way to say it—*parked on the moon.*"

Leon nodded. "You're trying to get there, yourself."

Caroline said, "I know. But I can't forgive myself. Or I've forgotten how, if I ever knew."

"You have to let God do it for you. By grace, He does for us what we can't do for ourselves. Like forgiving ourselves."

"But I feel like I don't deserve to be forgiven," Caroline said. "I can't forgive myself, because I know I don't deserve it."

"Really," Leon said, "no one deserves it, on their own merit. But by God's grace, it is possible. We have to ask for forgiveness, and then we have to trust God to do what He has promised He will do. Trusting God this way is an act of faith. And faith is the only thing we have to offer in this transaction."

"Forgiveness for killing a man?" Caroline asked.

"Yes," Shetler said. "It's that way for all of us. Outside of grace, we are powerless to forgive ourselves."

Caroline held her thoughts for a moment and then asked, "You've been talking about this type of thing with Darba?"

"Yes," Leon said, "going back a long time. Going back to when her troubles really began."

Caroline said, "I've known her for several years, but I don't think I know what Darba's troubles really are. At least I don't know how they started."

Cal said, "She has a mental imbalance, but it started one year when she was still teaching. She had a fourth-grade classroom in Fredericksburg."

"I didn't know Darba was a teacher," Caroline said. "That seems improbable, now."

"She was a good teacher," Katie said. "But she became troubled, and it went untreated. Then she snapped one day in class."

Cal explained. "One of her boys ran down to the principal's office, saying there was something wrong with Miss Darba. When they got down to her classroom, she had a little girl backed into a corner, screaming at her about not being a 'nosy little bossie.' They couldn't get her calmed down, and deputies and paramedics had to escort her out of her classroom."

Caroline argued, "Darba's troubled, but she's not mean like that."

"No, she's not," Leon said. "But she can't forgive herself for hurting that little girl. Dr. Carson treats her mental problems, but guilt is one of the things that Darba can't seem to shake."

"Darba didn't kill someone," Caroline whispered. "I'm sorry, but it's not the same."

"We are taught that we are to be harmless as doves," the bishop said. "It means a lot of things, but one thing is that the harm we do is always harmful to us, if for no other reason than the guilt that we shoulder for it. So, that's where forgiveness is necessary."

"I know I am not harmless," Caroline said.

The bishop nodded. "None of us is. That's why forgiveness is necessary."

"It's hard to accept," Caroline said. "It sounds so easy, but really it's hard."

"It may not be easy," the bishop said, "but it is simple. I was just getting Glenn Spiegle to understand that. I think maybe he was finally able to accept it."

"Forgiveness?" Caroline said.

"Yes."

"Then, what about people like Jacob Miller?" Caroline asked. "He apparently never even knew that he needed to be forgiven."

Shetler smiled sadly. "I spoke to Jacob, yesterday. I asked him what he thought it meant in the scriptures, where it reads, 'Behold, I send you out as sheep among wolves. Wherefore, be ye wise as serpents and harmless as doves.' I asked him if we are to be harmless as doves for the well-being of the wolves."

"What did he say?" Caroline asked.

"He had no reply," the bishop said.

"Wise as serpents *and* harmless as doves?" Caroline asked. "Both for *our* benefit?"

Leon smiled, "Doesn't that make sense to you, now that you know guilt? To be harmless spares us, first."

"And forgiveness is always possible?"

"Yes, if we will only ask."

"By grace?" Caroline asked, tears flowing again. "Not because we deserve it?"

"Yes," the bishop said and reached over the table to take her hands. "Outside of grace, forgiveness isn't possible. It might as well be parked on the moon."

* * *

Riding home later in Cal's truck, the storm over, Caroline called her husband. He asked how she was, and she said, "Better, Michael. I've been talking with Cal. And Katie and Leon Shetler."

"Are you still sad about Eddie?" the professor asked.

"A little, I guess. It's not so bad, now. Did they catch that Render?"

"No," Branden said, and he explained.

"Where are you now?" Caroline asked.

"We're at the hospital. Waiting for the doctors to let us talk with Stevens Clark."

"I don't remember who he is," Caroline said.

"He was driving Jacob Miller, when Render shot them. He's been through two surgeries, and now they think he can talk a little bit."

"Does he know where Render is?"

"We don't know," Branden said. "But if he doesn't, then nobody does."

"When are you coming home, Michael?"

"Tomorrow afternoon," Branden said. "We have a flight at five o'clock."

"Do you need me to pick you up?"

"At Akron/Canton," Branden said. "Gets in at seven-ten."

"What are you going to do until then?"

"If Clark tells us anything we can use, we'll go back after Render."

"I don't want you chasing this guy down, Michael."

"It'll be the sheriff or the Coast Guard. We'll hang back."

"Not the lead boat, Michael."

"No," Branden laughed. "Not the lead boat."

33

Friday, October 9
7:15 P.M.

WHEN ORTON, Niell, and Branden got to Stevens Clark's room in the surgical ward at Manatee Memorial Hospital in Bradenton, Clark was sitting in a padded chair beside his bed, fumbling with the red button on a gray metal box that controlled his pain medication. An IV line fed drugs into the back of his hand, and the right side of his face was bandaged heavily. He looked as haggard as battle fatigue, but he reacted strongly to the uniforms Niell and Orton wore, barking out, "I've got nothing to say! Leave me alone!" as he tried to stand. But his IV lines were tangled around his arm and in the clamps on their stand beside him, and after a frustrating attempt to unravel the lines, Clark flopped back in his chair and cursed the tubing for its stubbornness.

Branden stepped forward and said, "I can get that." Too frustrated to argue, Clark hung his head and surrendered his arm to Branden, muttering, "*Whatever.*"

Branden untangled the lines, and Clark stood up, sat on the edge of his bed, and fell back sideways on the mattress, grumbling, "We never should have gone out to Cortez."

Niell stepped to Clark's side and said, "We're looking for the man who shot you."

Clark eyed Niell's uniform and asked, "You're not local?"

"Holmes County, Ohio," Niell said.

Derisively, Clark shouted, "Wonderful! First Jacob Miller nearly gets me killed, and now you boys are gonna want to ask me stupid questions about the man who shot me."

"That's what we want to ask you about," Niell said. "Jacob Miller. How did he nearly get you killed?"

Clark laid his fingertips against the bandages on the side of his face and said, "These aren't chigger bites, Deputy."

Branden said, "I think what Sergeant Niell means is, 'What were you two doing when Jacob Miller nearly got you killed?'"

"Running!" Clark shouted and winced at the pain under his bandages. "We were running from Conrad Render."

"But why, Mr. Clark?" Ricky asked. "What did you do?"

"I didn't do anything," Clark complained. "It was all Miller. He came hotfooting it out of that warehouse and told me, 'Drive!' So I did. Made it over the bridge, got myself shot at the light, and don't remember much after that."

"Did Miller tell you why you were going to see Conrad Render?" Branden asked.

"Only thing he said was that he knew 'this fellow' was a bad man, and this was going to be *his big payday.* If I had known it was Conrad Render we were chasing, I'd never have been driving him around."

"You didn't know?" Ricky asked, surprised and not bothering to hide it.

"I just drove him where he said to go. He'd go in somewhere, and I'd wait in the truck. When he came out, he'd have someplace else for us to go. We chased all over like that, looking for him."

"When did he tell you it was Render?" the professor asked.

"He didn't," Clark said. "I didn't know he was looking for Render until I saw Old Connie pull up beside us at that intersection."

"You still sure it was Render?" Orton asked.

Clark gave a weary sigh, and muttered to himself, "I'm keeping the company of imbeciles." Then louder, he said, "I promise you boys. If I had known it was Render, I'd have just put a bullet in my own head, and saved myself the trouble of running for the rest of my miserable life."

Intending to encourage the man, Ricky said, "The sheriff has boats on the river, and the Coast Guard is patrolling the coastline and the bays. Someone will catch him."

Showing the fatigue of pain, Clark asked, "Don't nobody listen no more? He's not out on the water."

"I don't think you've told anyone that," the professor said.

"I'm telling you now! He's in a warehouse in Cortez! Beside one of the fish plants on the south side. He's holed up in a warehouse at the waterfront, where he can put his boat under cover. That's where Jacob Miller found him. In a waterfront warehouse in Cortez. We barely made it back over the bridge before he gunned us down!"

"Why haven't you told anyone?" the professor demanded.

Sighing heavily, Clark mumbled, "Morons," and looked around the room as if he were searching for an escape route. Then he said, "Because, boys, if you're really gonna go after him—*like really going to try to catch him this time*—then I need you to get him for sure. Otherwise I'm a dead man."

A nurse arrived with a stern expression and marched up to Clark's bedside, saying, "That's enough. Mr. Clark needs to settle down."

"Just a few more questions," Ricky insisted. "Just one or two more."

The nurse stepped back and folded her arms, saying, "I'll stay here. Two questions and then you'll have to leave."

"Are you sure he's still there?" Ricky asked. "Maybe he's cleared out by now."

"Warehouse! Waterfront! Cortez!"

"That's enough," the nurse stepped forward. "You're going to have to leave."

Standing fast, Ricky said to the nurse, "He can draw us a map."

"Morons!" Clark shouted. "Get me some paper."

34

Saturday, October 10

FIRST LIGHT

THE PROFESSOR attempted to train his binoculars in the general direction of the waterfront warehouse doors, but the rise and fall of Orton's thirty-foot skiff on Sarasota Bay lifted his line of sight up and down, and all Branden saw was rhythmic flash-by glimpses of the warehouse, as the skiff rode the chop on the water. They were tied at anchor over a sandbar, two hundred yards out from the warehouse, which fronted the water on massive wood pilings east of the big fish company's docks in Cortez. At water level, the warehouse presented a maze of enclosed docks, with articulated garage doors in front of each bay. Branden was struggling to hold his binoculars on the third bay from the left.

To the north, boats large and small strained on their moorings near the fishing pier at Bradenton Beach. A strong onshore wind cast a haze of salt spray over the turquoise water. A flight of five pelicans came gliding low over the water in front of the skiff, oblivious to the drama that was unfolding on the bay. All around the boat, whitecaps danced in front of the wind, as the sun came up over the trees to Branden's right, with an early morning promise of intensity and heat.

Between the skiff and Render's location stood three Coast Guard vessels, two of the fast orange RBSs and one of the larger UTBs. To the south, other boats blocked the routes to the Gulf through nearby Longboat Pass and at New Pass between Longboat and Lido Keys. To the west, two Coast Guard helicopters, deployed from the Clearwater station, hovered over the waters of Bradenton Beach, just offshore. The sheriff also had men in boats at the drawbridge to the north, clearing early fishing craft from the area, in case any of the action ran in that direction. The activity repeated to the southwest, in the popular waters around the drawbridge at Coquina Beach.

On land, approaching the warehouse from the north, the Manatee County sheriff's SWAT entry teams moved into positions on both sides of the warehouse. Sniper teams deployed on the rooftops of nearby buildings to the east and west.

Niell and the professor stood in the skiff forward of the wheel and Orton held a handset radio in the stern. "They'll make soft entries from the sides," he said. "Try to move people out of the building, before they close on Render."

The professor pulled his binoculars over to the west side of the building and caught a brief glimpse of a SWAT team lined up outside a door, while the lead man knelt to try the knob. When the chop on the water next allowed Branden to see that spot again, the last member of the team was moving into the building, with his weapon trained forward to let the sights of his gun track the movement of his eyes. When Branden had found the other side of the building, he saw that the eastside SWAT team, too, had made its entry into the building.

As Branden fought the rise and fall of the skiff, trying to keep his binoculars trained on the building, Orton shouted, "There!" Branden took the binoculars down from his eyes and saw that the third garage door from the left had shattered outward, as if a blast had taken it apart. Charging toward them, two hundred yards away, was Render's flame-painted cigarette boat, the wake behind his three outboard motors spraying thirty feet into the air.

Render came out straight toward Orton's skiff, the hull of his go-fast boat lifted up high to fly, only the engines at the stern engaging the water. Branden watched the fast boat close the distance at an astonishing speed, and guessing Render's intent, he knotted his fingers into the straps of Ricky's life vest, pulled him down beside him and shouted,

"Hold on to something!" just seconds before the orange and red flames of Render's painted hull strafed past the skiff. Before Branden could secure a grip in the skiff, Render sliced past them and crashed against the gunwales so violently that the skiff rocked on edge and cast the three men overboard.

Branden lost his grip on Niell's vest and was tossed several yards away from the skiff. He turned back to look for Ricky and saw that one of his shoes was hung up on a starboard gunwale cleat. Niell lay facedown in the water, with his leg held out of the water by the boat cleat. His limp body was knocking against the hull at the waterline, as the waves tossed the skiff up and down. Branden swam forward and kicked himself up to grab the high gunwale, but missed. He kicked again and caught hold of the cleat, but his fingers slipped as the waves tossed the boat up violently. He was thrown back into the water.

On his third attempt, Branden's grip held, and he pulled himself up enough to wrestle Niell's shoelaces free of the gunwale cleat, just before the next wave threw them both back from the skiff. Branden reached for Niell in the water and managed to turn him over. Neill coughed out water and gave a ragged groan, his arms floating limp at his sides. Branden tightened the straps at the neck of Niell's life vest so that the padded collar would best hold his face out of the water. Then he turned toward the skiff to look for Orton.

At the stern, Branden spotted the white deck shoes on Orton's feet just below the surface. The rest of Orton's body was somehow pinned beneath the outboard engine. Branden tried to pull himself underwater, but his vest kept him afloat. He worked the straps loose in front, struggled out of the vest, and kicked out of his shoes, as the waves tossed him up and down beside the stern.

He drew breath to dive underwater, but he was thrown against the driveshaft of the outboard engine. His forehead collided with the engine housing, and he tasted blood. He lay back and kicked away from the engine and floated on his back to catch his breath. Ignoring the gash over his eye, he rolled over, dove down, and swam forward underwater.

The straps of Orton's vest were tangled in the props. Orton's mouth was open, and his eyes were fixed with unconsciousness. With the engine and skiff lurching up and down, Branden surfaced and pulled Orton's dive knife out of its ankle sheath. Then he dove back underwater at the props and cut the straps of Orton's vest to free him. Losing air himself, and feeling his lungs burning, Branden dropped the knife, bunched his fingers onto Orton's collar, pushed away from the propeller shaft, and kicked for the surface.

* * *

Coast Guard seamen pulled Sergeant Orton out of the water and administered CPR until he coughed up seawater and spat out indignation. Flopped over onto his stomach and belching more water onto the deck, Orton struggled to curse out enough bravado to cover his embarrassment, but eventually he lay flat on his belly, happy just to breathe.

They handed Ricky Niell up to the deck of the UTB and then hoisted Branden, too. Ricky sat dazed on the deck of the boat, fumbling to unhook his life vest, but a bo'sun's mate stopped him, saying, "You're gonna want to leave that on, Sergeant."

When Ricky next saw Branden, he was back in a vest, too, so he stopped working on his straps and sat back to try to understand what had happened. He knew he was on the stern deck of one of the UTBs, and although his hearing was impaired, he could feel the vibration of the diesel engines beneath him. He wasn't quite certain how he had gotten there, but he knew to cling to the engine hatch as the boat picked up speed.

Branden stood up on the deck beside Niell, clutching the railing and trying to let his knees take the pounding of the deck, as he watched toward the south, where they had told him Connie Render had fled down the bay. He heard the radio squawking in the wheelhouse, and the captain responded by thrusting forward on the throttles to lift the boat up for speed. Soon they were pounding over the choppy water, spraying water and sea foam off the bow, racing in a long arching curve for the shoreline near Longboat Pass, where pleasure craft were gathering early for a lazy day in the shallows, several boats floating at anchor near the sandy beach, others pulled up on shore, with people in swimming suits carrying picnic supplies to land.

The UTB slowed near shore and broadcast emergency instructions for skippers to beach their boats and clear the channel. Another UTB came in behind and stood off in the channel, to help block the passage out to the Gulf. The professor's UTB then went on south toward the chase, and over the radio, Branden heard that the Coast Guard had managed to turn Render around at Lido Key. He was headed back north on Sarasota Bay, and orders to engage had been issued, giving permission to shoot at Render's engines, at which point the chase boats were ordered to back off and make way for the helicopters to come in low with their guns.

When he noticed Ricky trying to stand, Branden handed himself along the orange railing and helped Ricky up. Then, standing together in the stern, their view ahead blocked by the wheelhouse, they held onto the railing, trying to let their legs adjust to the pounding of the hull.

Their boat threw spray to starboard and maneuvered a tight turn a hundred yards offshore, at the northern tip of Longboat Key, and then the engines dropped to idle, and the stern lifted as the bow bit into the water and the UTB coasted to a stop.

From the south, white dots high over the water marked the positions of the helicopters. Beneath them, the men could see Render's go-fast boat careening to left and right, as it sped up the bay, trying to shake the helicopters trailing it.

The action came closer, Render flying over the water in front of the helicopters, and Branden and Niell could see Render's engines churning the water as he came forward, slashing close to other craft, rocking boats tied at their moorings, and spraying water as he swung back and forth, trying to evade the guns on the helicopters. But the helicopters drew steadily closer to Render, and one set up in front of Render, matching his speed, swinging left and right as it came on sideways toward the UTB carrying Niell and Branden.

Commands to stop blared from the helicopters as they chased the go-fast boat up the broad waters of the bay, but Render kept coming. Warning shots went into the water over Render's bow, and still he charged, engines screaming on a straight path now. The second helicopter came in to flank Render's boat and dropped low for a shot at the engines, the gunner hanging in a harness from the bay doors on the side of the helicopter. Still the cigarette boat came on, gathering speed where the waters grew smoother, and the gunner opened up on the engines with his slug gun, muzzle flashes and smoke thumping out of the barrel. The first rounds missed, and Render came forward. The helicopter drew down the distance, coming in to hover over Render's stern again, and a second volley of slugs pierced two of Render's engines, sending the boat careening to port, with only one engine still operating. Then another shot hit home, and Render's boat burst into a ball of flame and blew apart like a matchstick model, with a geyser of water pluming boat parts into the sky, before the charred hull fell back and sank on the spot where it had been taken.

35

Friday, October 16
10:05 A.M.

NEARLY A week later, on a cold Friday morning, Bruce Robertson stood at the north windows of his office and watched light snow settle around the Civil War monument at Millersburg's courthouse. He had just that morning printed guidelines from the Internet pertaining to proposals to the Department of Homeland Security for supplemental funding in law enforcement staffing. He had found the Internet files just as Rachel Ramsayer had taught him, and now that he was learning computers from an expert, he wondered what had been so hard about IT in the first place. Maybe Rachel was right. Once he got past his aversion to change, he could master computers as well as anyone could. So, I'll work on that, he thought. Take lessons from Rachel, get modern with the digital age, and bring some long-overdue changes to the sheriff's office.

Still standing at the window, Robertson heard Ellie come into the office, and he turned to watch her lay papers into the in-box on his desk. Smiling, he asked her, "Can you put any of that on our server?"

"I did some that way," Ellie said, smiling.

"Good," Robertson said. "I'll look at it later this morning."

Ellie studied the sheriff's expression for signs of mirth and decided that Robertson was serious. "I can put a lot of this paperwork on the server, Bruce. You wouldn't need to handle paper copies at all."

"Let's not get too crazy," Robertson smiled. "I don't want to frighten anyone."

"Still working with Rachel?" Ellie asked at the door.

"When she can fit me in," Robertson said. "Evenings, mostly, this last week."

Ellie nodded her approval. "Ricky and the professor are in the squad room. You ready for them?"

Robertson stepped to his desk and took the Homeland Security documents off the top of a stack of papers. He handed them to Ellie and said, "Bring 'em both in, Ellie. Ricky's had enough of a vacation. In the meantime, let me know what you think we can do with those supplemental programs from Homeland Security."

* * *

When Branden and Niell came into his office, Robertson was parked in front of a twenty-four-inch monitor, studying photographs that Sergeant Orton had transmitted from Bradenton Beach—boat debris floating on the water where Render's boat had exploded, and twisted engine parts that divers had brought up from the bottom of Sarasota Bay.

As Niell and Branden sat down, Robertson tapped the screen and said, "They pretty well blew this boat apart."

Seated, Niell said, "I'm surprised there's anything left of it. The gas tanks blew when they shot out the engines."

Robertson threw a few taps at his keyboard and looked up, saying, "Rachel is a genius. Once you have a decent monitor, you can actually use these things."

Niell and Branden exchanged bemused glances, and Branden asked, "Did they find a body yet?"

Robertson pushed back from his desk. "No. Orton doesn't think they will."

"Are you going to close the investigation?" Branden asked. "Into Spiegle's murder?"

"Haven't decided," Robertson said. "If I had a detective bureau, I'd stay on it a little longer."

Niell shrugged and said, "The one man who apparently knew it all was Conrad Render, and he went down with his boat."

Robertson stood and moved to the windows to watch the snow fall on the square. "I think Jacob Miller had figured it all out. Figured out that Render killed Spiegle and Winters. I think he went back down one last time to blackmail Conrad Render, and it got him killed."

"Probably," Branden said, "but we'll never prove it. Anyway, Vesta thinks her father was using Spiegle's past to pressure him. You know, *pay up or I'll tell Render where you are*. That sort of thing."

Robertson watched the snow for a moment and turned back to say, "Render might have found out Miller was asking around about Spiegle. Then, he could have just followed Miller up here and found Spiegle on his own. But, all in all, it's not a very satisfying wrap on the case. Spiegle's murder is going to have to go on the books as unsolved."

"You'd let it go like that?" Branden asked.

"Don't see that I have any choice," Robertson said. "Besides, the more troubling matter to me is how we blew it on Crist Burkholder's confession. Linda Hart pretty well handed me my hat on that one."

"I don't see what we'd have done differently," Niell said.

Robertson sat behind his desk again. "Ricky, if we had a detective bureau, don't you think we'd have processed Crist Burkholder more thoroughly? Maybe noticed that his hands weren't bruised?"

"I suppose so," Ricky allowed.

Robertson nodded. "Ellie's working on a grant proposal for me. We're going to try to expand, using Homeland Security grants. How'd you like to work with Pat Lance at the rank of detective?"

Niell looked to Branden and back to Robertson. "A detective bureau?"

Robertson buzzed his intercom and asked, "Ellie, can you make Ricky a copy of those Homeland Security guidelines?" Then to Niell, he said, "I want you to look over the guidelines, Ricky. I think we can get funding for this. I want to hire Rachel Ramsayer as a consultant, too. Have her on staff as IT chief."

Branden smiled and nodded to Ricky, "Detective."

"Anyway," Robertson said, as he stood. "Get the documents from Ellie, and let me know what you think."

Unsure what to say, Ricky pushed out of his chair, stepped to the door, and said, "Detective?"

Robertson said, "We made mistakes with Crist Burkholder, Ricky. I think we need a detective bureau. But, you let me know what you think, once you've studied the guidelines."

* * *

After Ricky had left, Robertson said to Branden, "Mike, you need to call Ray Lee Orton. He's been bugging me for your cell number."

"Why?" Branden asked, still thinking about Robertson's unexpected forward momentum with computers and detectives.

"He says he has a beach cottage, on Longboat Key," Robertson said. "He's grateful to you for saving his life, and he wants you to use the cottage whenever you need a vacation. Wants to send you a key to the place."

"He doesn't have to do that," Branden said.

"You should call him," Robertson said. "Take the cottage once in a while. You and Caroline could use a break."

"I teach," Branden said. "And in the summer, it'd be too hot in Sarasota."

"I was thinking maybe it was time for you to come down out of your ivory tower, Mike."

"And do what?" Branden asked. "Work for you?"

"Wouldn't be so bad," Robertson said. "You could work in my detective bureau."

"I'm a classroom teacher, Bruce," Branden argued. "I wouldn't know how to do anything else for a regular living."

"But, if I got a detective bureau," Robertson asked, "you'd consider it?"

"I'd still want to teach," Branden said.

"Seems to me," Robertson said, "that you've been doing both of these jobs, for the last couple of years, anyway."

Branden nodded. "But I don't think our new college president would like the idea very much—part-time teacher, and part-time detective—at least not at an official level."

"You've already been doing the work, Mike," Robertson said. "I'm just talking about giving you the title to go with that."

"I'm not sure that would work out, Bruce."

"Because of your new president?"

Branden nodded.

"Didn't you pretty much hire her?" Robertson asked.

"I chaired the committee that hired her," Branden said. "Then I went on sabbatical."

"Is she working out?" Robertson asked.

Branden shrugged. "Been on sabbatical, Bruce."

"Well, when you get back," Robertson said, "I hope to be able to offer you an official position."

"What would it pay?" Branden teased.

"Practically nothing," Robertson laughed. "You'd have to teach on the side, to earn a living."

Branden smiled and changed the subject. "How's it going, studying computers with Rachel?"

Robertson popped out of his chair. "Been great, Mike. But listen to this. I want to know if you've heard of this guy."

Then Sheriff Robertson punched *Play* on his CD rack, and an island rhythm with steel drums and an easy guitar was playing behind a singer who knew that *one particular Caribbean harbor.*

Branden smiled. "That's Jimmy Buffett."

"You've heard of him?"

"Yes, Sheriff. I've heard of Jimmy Buffett."

"Humpf," Robertson grunted out. "Rachel plays these songs when I go over to take lessons with her. Seems to relax me."

Branden laughed out loud, and Robertson asked, "What?"

"Jimmy Buffett and Bruce Robertson," Branden said. "Who'd have believed it?"

"He been around a while, Mike?"

"Oh, about fifty years, Sheriff."

"Well, I kinda like him."

"OK, then," Branden said. "I think I'll call Orton, after all."

"What changed your mind, Mike?"

"We'll take that cottage, after all, Sheriff. You and Missy, Caroline and me. We'll go down to Florida and find a Jimmy Buffett concert to go to."

"That'd be good, Mike. I think I'd like that."

36

Saturday, October 17
4:45 A.M.

THE BISHOP pulled the curtains back at his bedroom window and studied the vast spray of stars across the sky, thinking how lucky he was to see this every morning. How many men in America have this blessing, he asked himself? To see the stars from your own farm, ten miles from any human light that might dim this declaration of vastness. How many men knew about this blessing, to wake before most had ever dreamed of doing, and see the lights of night?

He pulled his string-tie blouse over his head, and stepped into his denim trousers. Next came his waistcoat, also of denim, stitched by his wife, sized so comfortably and broken in so softly as to be part of him, a part of his place on earth. How many men enjoyed the luxury of their wife's own sewing? How many enjoyed the blessings of the house they themselves had built? The bishop knew it was few, and he sighed. Sad, he thought. Sad how many men miss the true blessings.

In the kitchen, he lit his fire in the cooking stove and put on a kettle of water for his coffee. He stepped into his muck boots on the back porch, and then came back to stand in front of the fire, warming himself by the dancing flames, thinking they also were a blessing that too few knew.

When the water was hot, he poured it into a cup with his instant coffee crystals, and he gave it a stir with his callused finger. Cup in hand, he stepped off the back porch, and looked up again at the canopy of stars.

As he pulled his head back to see, he heard his milk cow stamping her hooves in the barn, and he thought, "There's

Hedda again, always in her stall ahead of me. Impatient old girl, I'm coming."

On his milking stool, Leon pulled the sweet milk from her and allowed his mind to start planning his day. Usually, he wouldn't allow this so early. He wouldn't worry his day forward too fast. But this was an unusual day. Crist and Vesta were home to visit with Crist's parents, and the bishop had business with them that he very much planned to enjoy.

But it is only because of the sadness, he reminded himself, that this is all now possible. Three men dead, and the murderer of them all sent to the bottom of Sarasota Bay. Sad, he thought, that they thought to play God with their lives, when all that was required of them was to do no harm. To be wise, and to do no harm.

But never mind the sadness, he thought. Later, after it is light, you'll go to Crist and Vesta. You'll explain to them that they are to have the Spiegle farm. Who else should have it, if not them? Who better to give it to? It was the blessings of a bishop to make these types of decisions, and Leon Shetler had savored the blessings of this gift since he first had considered it.

Before then, it had been a problem. People had been asking. What was to become of the Spiegle farm, now that it belonged to the bishop? Leon had nurtured this secret in his heart, since the day his wife Katie had suggested it. Why not give the Spiegle farm to Crist and Vesta? Keep them near to us, she had said. Help them, Amish or not, and maybe they will embrace the church someday.

The milking done, Leon carried his pail back into the kitchen and set it on the counter. Katie was up and making coffee for herself, so he sat with her and counted that a blessing, too. How many men knew to spend their time as wisely as this? To take your morning coffee with your wife, by firelight, and let your day come forward on its own time.

Not so many men knew to do that, the bishop mused. Not so many men at all.

37

Sunday, October 25
2:00 A.M.

BILLY CAME home to Darba in the darkest of the night. He slipped into the house through the kitchen door off the back porch and found her sitting in the dark on the living room sofa. He knelt in front of her on the carpet and pulled her to him, her knees to either side of him, and he held her head on his shoulder until he felt her tears wetting his neck. Time and time again, he stroked her hair, and then he eased her away a little to look into her eyes, before he drew her close again.

Through her tears, Darba whispered, "I knew you weren't dead, Billy Winters. I would have felt you go."

Billy put his hands on the sides of her face and kissed her. "We've got to get out of here, Darba," he said. "We can't stay."

"I don't really think I can leave, Billy," Darba said.

"I know, Darba. But we've got to disappear."

"Just give me a minute," Darba whispered and pulled him into her embrace.

"They all think I'm dead," Billy whispered.

"I know, Billy. Not me."

"I want them all to keep thinking that way."

"Where are we going? We can't just disappear."

"That's just what we're gonna do," Billy said. "Disappear."

Darba sat back and held Billy's hands in her lap. "How did you get away, Billy?"

"First, we've got to get going. While it's still dark."

"No, Billy. You tell me first. You tell me how you got away, so I can believe you're really here."

Taking a seat on the sofa beside her, Billy said, "Connie pulled a knife on me, so I pulled a gun on him."

"Then what?" Darba asked. "You just ran away?"

"As fast as I could run," Billy smiled.

"But he cut you."

"Just a little."

"Where'd you go, Billy?"

"Darba, I was raised down there. I guess I still know a few places where old Connie couldn't find me."

"He's dead, Billy."

"No, he's not."

"How do you know?"

"I just do."

"What if you're wrong?"

"Darba, we have to assume I'm right."

"Because he'll come after you?"

"Yes. If he thinks he can find me."

"Is that why we have to go?"

"That's part of it. We have to go tonight."

"Where?"

"You remember how sometimes it took me a little longer to drive home from Florida?"

Darba nodded a puzzled yes.

"I've been looking for a place for us, where the government can't find us."

"And where Conrad Render can't find us?"

"Yes, Darba. I found a little farm in Virginia. On top of a mountain, so far back in that we'll always be safe."

"We're gonna live there?"

"We're going to hide there, and let the whole world think I'm dead."

"You mean let Conrad Render think you're dead?"

"The whole world, Darba. They all have to think I'm dead, because they all think I was carting drugs up here in the door panels of my truck."

"But you weren't."

"I know. But that won't matter to the Feds."

"How'd the drugs get there, Billy?"

"Connie put them there, after I ran away. To frame me."

"We could just tell them all that."

"Do you really think anyone would believe us?"

"No."

"Right."

"I'll miss the kids, Billy."

"They have kids in Virginia. You can learn to care about them."

"What about Dr. Carson?"

"They have psychiatrists in Virginia, too."

"When are we leaving?"

"Tonight. But you can't pack anything that someone might notice is missing."

"Like what?"

"Cell phones. Photographs. Keepsakes."

"Clothes?"

"We can take a few clothes. We'll buy more after we settle up for that farm."

"Who's gonna sell us a farm, Billy? We don't have any money. We don't have any way to hide who we really are."

"Wait," Billy said and pulled a penlight out of his jeans pocket. Then he pulled something thin out of his jacket pocket. When he shined the light into his hand, Darba saw two Virginia driver's licenses, one with Billy's picture and one with hers.

"Darba," Billy said, switching off the light. "We're gonna have new names."

"Are those forgeries?"

"Of course."

"Where'd you get them?"

"I guess I know some folks in Virginia. They don't like the government any more than I do. They take care of their own."

"Do they take care of people like us, Billy?"

"Yes, Darba. They live *off the grid*. Like we're gonna do."

"But we can't afford a farm, Billy. Where would we get that kind of money?"

Billy smiled, put the driver's licenses back in his pocket, and took Darba's hands in his. "We have the money, Darba.

It's hidden in the barn. I helped Glenn Spiegle bring it up here from Florida. It's cash money from his dead mother, and there's a lot of it."

"I don't understand," Darba said.

"Every time I went down there, I visited Glenn in prison. And I'd go out to see his mother. She'd give me several thousand in cash to bring up here, for when Glenn got out of prison. She knew she'd be dead by the time he got out, and she didn't want anyone to know that Glenn got so much of her money."

Darba smiled. "He'd be happy to know that we used it to start new lives."

"Yes, Darba," Billy said, "I think he would."